Dancing
with
MY DADDY

Dancing
with
MY DADDY

EVERY DAUGHTER'S JOURNEY

VALERY MURPHY

From my girlfriends...

PASTOR SHARON KELLY, WAVE CHURCH, VIRGINIA BEACH, USA

I am delighted that my friend Valery has penned this magnificent book, *Dancing with My Daddy*. In it she explores the wonderful relationship we can have with our heavenly father, and draws comparison from her own relationship with her dad. Though not a perfect relationship, Valery has asked the tough questions, and worked through the issues many of us face when we try and reconcile our earthly dad with our heavenly one. Her message is honest, and open and challenges us all to pursue an incredible relationship with our Father God!

CHRISTINE CAINE, EQUIP AND EMPOWER MINISTRIES

There is no doubt that the relationship between a daughter and her earthly father profoundly influences her perspective of her heavenly one. By beautifully sharing her own journey Valery shows that whatever your experience has been with your own father, there is a perfect Father in heaven who loves, values, adores, & delights in you. It is in His image we are created, restored & perfected.

PASTOR BOBBIE HOUSTON (HILLSONG)

This comes as a note of introduction and endorsement for Pastor Valery Murphy, as she presents her new book *Dancing with My Daddy*. My husband Brian and I have known Michael and Valery Murphy for 25 years. They were on our team and were our Associate Pastors for 12 years before going to pastor their own church in south Sydney.

Valery is a gracious and godly woman, of impeccable character and I am confident that this her first book, will open the human soul and connect the reader with the grace and goodness of God. Her manner is warm and wonderfully embracive.

DARLENE ZSCHECH, WORSHIP LEADER AND PASTOR
I am so thrilled that our beautiful friend Valery has finally written the first of the books that have been in her heart for so long. She has served God faithfully for so many years both with all of us at Hillsong church, Sydney Australia, and more recently as senior pastors in what has become a cutting edge, dynamic church in the South of Sydney. I am confident that *Dancing with My Daddy* will be like LIFE to many of you who read it...as Valery's honest but warm way of communicating truth has always been one of her incredible strengths. I pray your heart will find peace as you draw courage and dignity from this stunning story... Thank you Valery, shine on lovely one.......
With so much love, DARLENE

Published by Infl uence Resources
1445 N. Boonville Ave., Springfi eld, Missouri 65802

Published in association with The Quadrivium Group—Orlando, FL
info@TheQuadriviumGroup.com

Interior formatting and jacket design by Anne McLaughlin,
Blue Lake Design, Dickinson, Texas
Edited by James Stokes
Cover photo: www.andrewjamesphotography.com.au
Cover photo model: Molly Thistlewaite

ISBN: 978-1-93669-989-6

FOR MY FAMILY

To Dad and Mum—thank you for bringing us to this great country.

To my husband Michael. Thank you for your constant encouragement. You have always believed in me. Your love for me and our children is one of the most important things in my life. I love you forever.

To our three children, Leah, Ryan and Elyse. .

Leah—your help has been invaluable. From reading my book to actively supporting and advising me … Thank you for not letting me give up!

Ryan—so many "keep going Mum" hugs! Thanks for the cuppas…and the legal advice!

Elyse—Your cheering me on has meant the world to me, and your new understanding now of soldiers at war has amazed me.

And to my son in law, Andrew—thank you for capturing in a picture what was in my heart.

To my brother, James. I could not have written this book without your amazing help. Thank you for living it with me.

To our incredible, amazing church, Shirelive—you are loved beyond words.

And to my Daddy, whom I call "Abba"—thank you for being the very life I breathe….

Thank you Dr. Sam Chand, Debbie and Dream Releaser Publishing for your help in getting me started on the road to seeing my project launched!!

CONTENTS

INTRODUCTION

"As we stepped onto the floor, my heart was swept up by the lilting music. It had always had that effect on me. Music moved my young spirit and made my feet want to dance. Now as daddy cradled my small, vulnerable hand in his and we were away, I felt pulled into the rhythm of the song, carried along as though by a gentle wave in the ocean on the sunniest of summer days."

"A woman's relationship with her father is a training ground for all future relationships. Now psychologists say that the father-daughter relationship has far more to do with adult adjustment than was thought". *

The vital role played by the relationship between father and daughter is often hindered by life's hurts and difficulties. The protection, nurture and covering originally intended often goes awry, and daughters, because of this, find themselves measuring God with the measure shaped by their earthly dad. And so we as daughters are often left with a feeling of being incomplete. A feeling of having no role model of fatherhood that we are content with. We may feel the need to reach out and make our fathers someone that they never were, or ever could be.

For the daughter who has suffered abuse at the hand of a father, who has been left with shattered dreams and hopes because of the under-valuing of herself in the eyes of perhaps the most important person in her life, a relationship with the Heavenly Father can release her untapped potential, helping her to flourish in a beautiful and releasing way. Only He has the ability to wipe away the hurt, the negative images and the damage that may have been impressed upon her.

For the daughter whose father was loved and revered, whose relationship with him was untainted and remembered with fondness, the bond with our Heavenly Father can secure and establish her heart, deepening the trust that has started here on Earth, continuing the beauty and the love that a Daddy can bring. But now it becomes Eternal. The Bible speaks of the character of God being loving, kind and gentle, just, merciful and righteous. He is rescuer, friend, confidant and lover. Because of experience in life we often find it hard to imagine that this could be true.

I have captured here some of the memories of a father who is long gone from this Earth. Many facets of his character and his life were probably yet to be developed. So I had the opportunity to see only what the heart and mind of an immature little girl can hold and cling to, of a man whose life was painfully, yet quickly lived. Memories can be cherished or erased, depending on the depth of pleasure or pain that they produce. So much of what I recall as the attributes of a father are not what I have come to know as belonging to my Heavenly Father.

My dad died when I was a teenager. During his life no matter what his weaknesses, as his daughter I only ever wanted to see his strengths. I needed the power of my protector and my rescuer. But life stole his sanity, because of his war-torn heart and mind. The trauma of conflict caused him to become a shadow of the man that God created him to be. It took away his intimacy, and caused him to retreat into himself.

Recovery from that came at a price, a toll on his physical, mental and emotional health. Stability was stolen in increasing measure. A change of geography from one side of the world to the other, a new country and culture, a job which was promised but did not exist. Gradually the ability to provide adequately for his family disappeared, and with it his male pride. Dignity, the right of every man, was ripped from him along with his sense of self worth and the ability to control his own life. Replaced with an uneasy dependence on others, this resulted in a frustration that grew with the years. Life stole from my earthly father. He was not perfect.

This is every daughter's journey, the search to find the perfect Father. He waits to be found. As you read the chapters, you will notice that I have provided some reflections at the end ("Think About This") and then some suggestions about how we can use the lessons in each story to impact and perhaps apply change in our own lives, even though we may or may not have lived through similar experiences.

In "Over To You" the scriptures have been used to give comfort and assurance in going forward, and then perhaps you could join in the prayer with me at the end of each chapter. I pray that you will find in these pages not only poignant and sometimes heart warming stories, but that each page will bring a new closeness for you to the One who loves you more than you love yourself:

Your Daddy in Heaven.

L to R: British Army registration, Dad with two soldier friends in India in 1930's, POW camp band with drummer Harry, POW Stalag IIIA (Germany) program, Valery at age four, Musical Program – POW camp, Valery age 5 – school photos!

THE OLD COUNTRY

I was born in England. It was the post World War II years, and the country was recovering from the overwhelming experience of a fight for its very existence as a free nation.In the hearts of many of its people there was also an inner battle that still raged and would continue, as individuals tried to build families and lives upon the rubble and ruins of broken heart and spirit.

The freedom on the inside that England's people needed was now to become a personal journey that would affect the generations. Particularly in the heart of the fathers, there would be a daily struggle to overcome the pain and the memories that lingered, ever vivid. Haunted by the tragedy of war, its casualties would continue to limp and to live their lives under a personal shadow of wounds that were concealed but still very real. Hampered personally by the rejection and injustice that many had endured during years in Prisoner of War camps in Europe, Britain's fathers fought now the inner battles of the heart, in order to survive as well adjusted and loving human beings. In the "Old Country" many ex-soldiers and their families played out a familiar story.

Wartime Relic

Power Over Past Hurts

It didn't glint in the sun. No more than a sharp, dull-grey, very thin rectangular piece of tin. Light in my hand. Yet I felt the weight of the years written into it, and I knew the significance of its history. As my brother handed it on to me, I recognised the World War II prisoner of war 'dog tag' that I had seen many years before. A reminder of dad and the secrecy of his past, the piece of metal meant little to anyone else in the room. I was alone and detached in the significance of the moment. My three children were caught up in a wave of laughter with their two cousins at a competitive game of snooker. My husband sat relaxed in an armchair, reading the sports page of a local newspaper. And in the midst of it, here was my brother handing me one of the most thought-provoking objects that I had ever seen.

It cowered in my hand with an air of mystery, relying on its very insignificant appearance to cover the dark secret of which it spoke. Man's inhumanity to man. A very silent witness. But its message was loud. Piercing. Its story spoke of a history of blood and sacrifice in which my father had been involved....

The year was 1940. In the chill of the morning the job seemed to be impossible. It was to load the remainder of this vast company of defeated British soldiers onto domestic, fishing and commercial craft, many of which seemed to list dangerously through overloading. Soldier assisted soldier as they scrambled aboard and turned to head that night from this beach in France to the shores of England on the other side of the English Channel. Swiftly and with determined resolve, the newly recruited volunteer 'captains' of the Home Guard sailed and navigated their frail little boats and exhausted human cargo to freedom. Visibility was only by the light of the moon. Yet each one knew that this was more than another fishing trip, more than another short crossing. This was a statement about victory: "never surrender" was the cry on the wind that night.

I wonder what each man held in his mind there, exhausted in every way from months of combat, poor diet and declining morale? I wonder what tricks of imagination lurked in the shadows of their thoughts? Thoughts of home, perhaps, so near but of course so far in the unpredictability of war. Thoughts of wives, sweethearts, children. And other beckoning, fleeting things that swirled in the mind but which could never be allowed to take up residence, just illegal squatters that struck a strange fear in the heart. Uninvited intruders. Perhaps memories never again to be experienced.

*As they boarded the waiting boats, many a soldier quieted him-
self, permitted at last to consider those comforting images so long
suppressed. Yet there were still many men of the infantry left fighting the enemy's front line soldiers as the others beat that hasty
retreat out to sea behind them. Valiantly they protected the escaping thousands. Bravely to defend their countrymen, they fought
until reduced to many less. Of this brave and essential rear guard,
some were later moved down the French coast to a small village
where the Dunkirk evacuation could be successfully repeated. The
remaining Allied troops could regroup on safer ground and from
there resist the advancing Blitzkrieg that was by now capturing
the freedom of the European continent.*

Or that's what had been hastily planned in the midst of confusion. For the 10,000 troops that waited in vain on the beaches of St
Valéry en Caux, this operation was unfortunately to have a very different and unintentional outcome. My Dad was there. Amongst the rear
guard at the battle of Dunkirk, it was by Providence's hand that he
was captured but not killed during the surrender of troops in this little
French village, St Valéry, in June, 1940. Because the story was rarely
and sketchily told, I had relied on my mother to fill me in during her
later years. But I do know that after his capture he became a prisoner
of war in a Nazi German camp. In fact, he became a prisoner of war
six times over.

Those times must have been an interminable nightmare, the kind
that recurs night after night until you awake, startled and covered in
sweat, not quite believing that you are in the real world. I know that
he was sent down to the German coalmines to work. He escaped seven

times, each time to be again captured and brought back to yet
another prison and yet another
angry commandant. The years
dulled what must have been in-
tense pain and the journey to the
edge of emotional and physical
health, a journey that was at once
fraught with outlandish fear, but
with also a pin hole light of hope.

Those times must have been an interminable nightmare, the kind that recurs night after night until you awake, startled and covered in sweat, not quite believing that you are in the real world.

It was that skerrick of light that must have sustained the young soldier, knowing that this hell of an existence could not possibly last. It could never be permitted to dull the senses, or you were finished. Your light would be most certainly fast extinguished if you gave in.

Once questioned about what he intended to do now that he had been recaptured, his answer was decisive, and I can just imagine the angle of that proud chin, the deepening of colour in those dark eyes, the resolve of a steady but determined look at the commanding officer with the answer:

"I'm just going to escape again!"…..

As dad was knocked senseless by the guard, somehow the inner man had grown in strength. And now as I turned the little piece of metal in my hand, caressing it and smiling to myself, I remembered the strength of will that was my father.

As a child I used to think that his moods were curious, and I could never figure out what could possibly have depressed him so. But since that time having researched his past and times, I can forgive the reactive behaviour, the anger and resentment that caused so much of what must have been going on in that mind—those hidden phantom thoughts that had forged the fiery conflicts in his life. For it seems that on that summer's day in 1940, though the rescue of the 10,000 men had been planned and supposedly was to have been carried out like a second Dunkirk operation, it failed miserably.

They stood on the shore at St Valéry, filled with the hope and anticipation of yet another daring rescue mission by that frail armada . All would be well, all would be taken care of by those commanding officers who had charge of their lives, those expert in such a mission whom they had learned implicitly to obey in military fashion. Confidence was theirs; they would indeed be home soon.

The reality, however, has been poignantly portrayed in the words of a song that stirred my heart when I read it. Those men were left abandoned.

When I returned at the end of the war,
From the Stalag where I'd been confined,
I read of the battles the allies had fought,
Stalingrad, Alamein, and the Rhine.
And with pride in their hearts people spoke of Dunkirk
Where defeat had become victory
But nobody mentioned that Highland Division.
They'd never heard of St.Valéry

No stories, no statues for those that were killed.
No honours for those who were gone.
Just a deep sense of shame as though we were to blame,

Though I knew in my heart we were not.
So I've moved to a country I've come to call home
But my homeland lies far o'er the sea.
I will never return while my memory still burns
On the beaches of St. Valéry. [1]

Recently, my family and I visited a fascinating memorabilia display and military museum in Scotland. Wondering why ever we had made the trip up there on that family holiday with our three now adult children, we were surprised to discover as we drove those tiny, hedge-lined hilltop roads, a beautiful, historic castle in the stunning Scottish village of Stirling.

Centuries ago this same castle had seen much of the romantic and swashbuckling history of the royal Stuart family, but now it was being taken care of by the military. And this chance discovery of mine was only to be the beginning of an amazing turn of events. A dusty spiral staircase led to an upper room where we discovered a fascinating display of materials collected from the British army's 51st Highland Division. Like a slow-motioned movie unraveling its plot, it dawned on me that this very regiment had been the one that my Dad had served with early in World War II.

As I looked around at the glass cases which housed so many memories and precious remnants of years ago, I realised that I was being presented with evidence of the entire story; the battle fought and lost at St Valéry en Caux, in the summer of 1940. This then, was the root of the conflict in his soul. Someone once said, "poor is the country with no heroes; and worse yet is the country that forgets them". Like

---

1   By an unnamed returned soldier, 51st Highland Division.

a forgotten hero, my father had become one of those lost between the pages of military history, whose sacrifice and service appear to be more of an embarrassment than a celebration. Feeling unappreciated and distressed, he'd never known where to put his anger and resentment. His smouldering indignation had grown with every year of torment, remembering the events that had ripped apart his life and future on that French beach.

There appears to be no solace and relief for the one who feels such lack of recognition. The history of the battle has been recorded, but many who were involved there still feel that they were deserted, abandoned on a cold and lonely beachhead, that dark day in June. There's a number on the face of the little grey piece of tin that I hold in my hand:

Stalag XX1B

That's all. The only thing written on my Dad's 'dog-tag' is a number. This little relic conveys so much, and yet records so little. And now I look at it with different eyes, with some belated but inadequate insight into the de-humanisation of life itself that is inflicted during war. On the face of the dog-tag there is just a number. What gives the soldier the sheer grit needed to continue to scheme and pull off an escape—not once, not twice—but seven times? It's that little pin-hole of hope, I suspect. That little glimmer of the future holding a life that is different. That iron will and determination to live in a better world. Thank God that my dad did not lose his hope after escape number six. For I would never have been born! It was after the ending of World War II that my Dad met his beautiful Kathleen back in England.

Dad, thanks for going back for a seventh try! To me it meant life itself. If there's one thing I've learned from you, it's this: when all else looks impossible, there is something within the human spirit that continues on if we will just let it rise. If we will look up and reach for Someone outside ourselves.

I would like to be able to write that this 'war hero' managed to get to a place in his life that reflected a reconciliation in his heart, such injustice having been laid to rest. But I am his daughter. I had to live with the results, the 'fall-out' that was his lack of emotional stability in the years that were to follow this period of his life. Those years included his marriage and his two children, and developed into a story that is littered with scenarios that often got so out of control.

Peace at home reigned only in short, unfamiliar bursts. Family was injured in the crossfire. Wounds of this 'war' took their toll, and betrayal was buried in hearts as we limped on the crutches of the day-to-day. Our concept of life was like a soldier's memories of the battle. We became encased in a tangle of scars that cried out to be healed. It seems that in every war the stories of the forgotten ones get locked away in the drawers of history, 'done and dusted'. Perhaps on examining the individual stories and giving recognition to the people involved we can help them to feel the value that they need to come to terms with, before it's too late. *That is, before their misunderstanding of themselves becomes imprinted upon another generation and its children.*

THINK ABOUT THIS:

There's a war been declared over our lives. It's one that will take us to the very 'edge' if we will let it. It manifests often in the battle we have with unforgiveness and regret. Wherever there is a rejection, there needs to be forgiveness. It could be towards another, towards ourselves, or towards God. We need the power of our Heavenly Father to help us to forgive those you feel don't deserve it, those who have hurt us because they themselves are hurting. It's impossible to try and do it alone.

There's a war been declared over our lives. It's one that will take us to the very 'edge' if we will let it. It manifests often in the battle we have with unforgiveness and regret.

OVER TO YOU:

Talking with a friend will often bring a healing and a 'way out' of the constant thoughts and uneasiness of the heart that plagues us because of what has gone before, or the heritage of rejection that we live with. How much better to bring it before the Healer of the human heart who loves you and is only a word away?

Forgiveness is hard, but as simple as a decision.

Is there someone who needs *your* forgiveness today?

Let's talk to Him who can heal the hurts and get rid of the anger and pain. If you read these scriptures, they say it all. Then, talk to the One who can help.

If you, like my dad, have experienced in life the abandonment and injustice that has left you feeling vulnerable and alone, there is One who understands our humanity, who can bring His healing touch to any situation.

As you continue to read and to reflect, let this truth be what helps you to undo the past hurt, to bring it into His Light, and allow the past to become much less influential in your daily life.

Psalm 102:1

Hear my prayer, O LORD, And let my cry come to You

Psalm 86: 5-7

O Lord, you are so good, so ready to forgive,

So full of unfailing love for all who ask your aid.

Listen closely to my prayer, O Lord;

Hear my urgent cry.

I will call to you whenever trouble strikes,

And you will answer me.

Ephesians 4:31

Get rid of all bitterness, rage, anger and harsh words, and slander, as well as all types of malicious behaviour. Instead, forgiving one another, just as God through Christ has forgiven you

Father in Heaven,

I am aware that forgiveness is not easy. In fact, there are and have been times when I am unable to forgive, for whatever reason. But now I am bringing to you my heart and my mind, and ask that you would help me to step past rejection, on to forgiveness of those that have hurt me. Lord, I give this burden to you. Amen.

2 Hidden In a Coal Cupboard

The Lonely and Abandoned Heart

Crouching down lower in an effort to make myself invisible, I covered my ears with tiny hands. It made the noise more bearable. I was around three or four years old, and my world was under attack. If it had been a quiet and colourful meadow before, now it was becoming a grey and ugly battleground.

Angry accusations from my mother had been countered by sharp, loud and aggressively defensive and abusive words from my father; and, though I desperately wanted it to stop, the argument continued. I had slipped into the small cupboard under the stairs, retreating when I had felt that another confrontation between my parents was approaching. Like a port in a storm to a tiny, weather-beaten dinghy, any hiding place would do, any retreat from the approaching tempest.

It wasn't unusual, but each time it happened I was more frightened, more insecure and more removed from the trust that I had placed in them. Sobbing, shaking and distraught in that tiny space, my heart was breaking. Behind the door I was safe. Distance put between me and them gave me my security. I wished and wished harder that my Mother would stop answering him. Maybe if she said nothing it would not anger him so much! But the storm continued to rage, and I shut my eyes, trying to imagine not even being there.

But the storm continued to rage, and I shut my eyes, trying to imagine not even being there.

My heart skipped a beat as I heard the words heading for the inevitable crescendo. I couldn't see my parents through the crack in the door, but then I heard a quick, sharp slap on skin and a piercing scream. Voices rose on a massive wave that climaxed and crashed as a door slammed shut nearby. I felt the vibration in the floor. Then quiet, and it became calm. The storm had subsided. I strained my head closer to the door—but there was silence. My little heart's beat was slowing now, my breathing becoming less shallow.

It seemed like hours that I stayed there, trembling and afraid to leave the security of my hiding place. I had lost a part of me that was to be hidden for many decades, buried in the small cupboard under the stairs. That part was my trust and my confidence in my father.

It must have been a year or so later. I remember mum pushing a dressing table against the bedroom door. As she pushed with all the strength that she could muster, breathlessly she tried to reassure me with short bursts of confident words that all would soon be ok, that the storm would soon pass. How could this be him? My image of daddy had been betrayed yet again, the picture shattered in the heart of this daughter. At times I would feel like a discarded rag doll, for surely the fault was mine. I must have been the cause of the conflict. I must surely have done some bad thing to make daddy so angry. In a man whose mind had been tormented by the horrors of war, the anger surfaced sometimes with only the slightest provocation. Sometimes unsettled by just a single word, he would soon be on a relentless path of anger, violence and destruction.

Those episodes of anger would overtake dad for days. Broodingly, concealed in the darkness, he would sit alone, with the only light coming from his constantly lit cigarette. He would live there with his demons, giving in slowly to their unrelenting pursuit of his mind, until he could fight no more. Surrendering to the enemy of depression, he would lay down his weapons in defeat: his mind taken captive by dark thought; his spirit now laden with hopelessness; his very motivation for living under siege. Love was lost to him in these times. And his little princess, approaching him sometimes with the innocence of childhood, would interrupt his solitude and melancholic thoughts with pleasantries that were cruelly cast aside. Not understanding the rebuff, her heart would slowly retreat from the relationship—a crusty hardness starting to spread over the once soft sands of a gentle, tender spirit.

From this I learnt rejection, the dejection of abandonment and the sorrow of a broken heart. My earthly dad was at the mercy of his own inadequacies, and his moods were constantly dictated by his own experiences. His efforts to rise above the brokenness of his own life were often fruitless and mostly misunderstood. He continued to walk the well-worn paths of his difficult life in the very best way he knew how. But habitually he fell helpless victim to this behaviour over and over again. This man who had partnered with the beautiful Kathleen to give me life; this man who had held me and loved me, named me and cherished me in his own way, still lives in my heart. My honouring of dad is never in question, but he carried an injured heart, and this affected his ability to show love at times. In effect, his wounds on the inside were played out in a life overshadowed by his own abandonment. This is so often the story, repeating itself over generations.

THINK ABOUT THIS:

For those daughters who have suffered abuse at the hand of a father, who have been left with shattered dreams and hopes because of the undervaluing of themselves in the eyes of perhaps the most important person in their lives, a relationship with the Heavenly Father can release untapped potential, helping her to flourish in a beautiful and releasing way. Only He has the ability to wipe away the hurt, the negative images and the damage that may have been impressed upon her. An 'invisible ceiling' restricts a daughter who feels abandoned and rejected. It needs to be shattered. A new daughter longs to emerge and to take hold of her life, unfettered and free to pursue this life as an individual, not as a product of someone else's insecurity or sin.

OVER TO YOU:

Perhaps from your own experiences you know the deep pain of suffering and rejection. Believe the Truth, which sets us up for a new and positive future. The Truth is that your Heavenly Father is not subject to human failings. He will not let you down.

If we use those negative experiences of our past to influence our future in a negative way, we will continue to bring ourselves pain.

If we use those negative experiences of our past to influence our future in a negative way, we will continue to bring ourselves pain. 'Justifying' our implosive or explosive behaviour will hamper and lengthen our search for who we "really" are. Perhaps it's time to evaluate our own hearts in the light of our experiences, and to ask for help to calm our own personal storm, so that we can in turn help others?

Matthew 28:20(b)

And be sure of this: I am with you always, even to the end of the age.

Psalm 107:29

He calmed the storm to a whisper and stilled the waves.

Psalm 62:8

O my people, trust in him at all times. Pour out your heart to him, for God is our refuge.

Heavenly Father,

Sometimes the 'storms' in my life rage out of control, leaving me with a feeling of wanting to 'hide'. Help me to see through the storm to the peace on the either side. Release me from the memories of the storms, and the after effects of the damage. Amen

3 Try a Little Tenderness

Awakened by Kindness

Dad used to love the Big Band style of music. So I got to know at an early age many of the hits of this wonderful, musical era from around World War II. One of his favourites was a song called "Try a Little Tenderness". It was unusual when we discovered anything in him that exposed raw emotion. So, all things considered, tenderness was not really something that he showed very often; except one day that stands out clearly in my memory.

It must have been when I was around eight years old. I was struggling to open my eyes. For a moment or two the blurry picture of someone's face, quite close. I shut my eyes again, reeling with dizziness. Opening them a few moments later I tried to see, feeling as though I was looking through a fog, but this time all was a little clearer. It was dad. Concern clouded his expression, furrowing his olive-skinned brow. As he saw recognition in my eyes, a smile crept from the centre of his mouth to lighten up his entire face, and he turned and called to Mum:

"Hurry, she's come to!"

He continued to dampen my face with a cloth, gently stroking down from forehead to cheek. Lovingly, softly, as only a parent can. I searched his big dark eyes for answers as to why I was here, what had happened. I had remembered nothing. But his gaze assured me, strengthening my trust and soothing the anxiety that had begun to try to envelop my heart. I became more awake with every movement, and started to half groan the words:

"Where am I, Dad?"

He told me the whole story with a slow, strong voice, coaxing me back to full consciousness as he went through what had gone on that morning after I had left the house, roller skates in hand, to play outside in the street. The cat that lived next-door to us had recently given birth to yet another litter of kittens. Not that I minded them, but sometimes I was a bit afraid of these furry little creatures. Adorable as they were, they were like miniature playful tigers! In fact, I had noticed that one particular little ginger ball of fluff loved to hide behind people and jump out at them when they least expected it! Trying out its sharp little claws in an effort to become the grown-up hunter that it one day longed to be, this cute and cuddly animal, I am sure, believed himself to be more than was evident right now—a veritable warrior just waiting for the chance to show his ferocity!

The week before, that very kitten had demonstrated this to me as I'd visited my neighbour friend, and she'd told me all about the new arrivals in the shed out back. Little girls seem to love fluffy kittens, but after the experience of being scratched repeatedly as I tried to treat this one like a baby, cradled in my arms, I was a bit wary. So as I had donned my roller skates for a morning of riding to fill in the time before lunch, I was unaware in skating down to my favourite lamp post (it was a steep hill and the post always stopped me just in time) that the same kitten was hiding behind it ready to jump playfully out at the next passer-by.

I still don't remember any of what went on that morning until I woke up in the lounge room on the couch, in the tender care of my dad. Now he recounted to me how I had been frightened by the kitten jumping out at me and had fallen heavily, hitting my head on an iron drain in the footpath. Seeing me from the kitchen window, our neighbour had carried me into our house unconscious. What thoughts of dread must have raced through both my parents' minds, as I lay there not moving, obviously injured and having been exposed to some danger.

As my father cared for me that day, I know that the only thoughts that were foremost in his mind were those of caring, rescue and protection. He proved to me by his actions that he was no different to my Father in the Heavens, who, I later was to discover, will always be there to rescue and to care, no matter what. It is the instinct of a parent to care for their child. Sometimes this basic reaction is thwarted, often involuntarily, by a parent who is themselves injured. But often it is true that care for their offspring transcends any thought for themselves or any concern about how they may be feeling; and all energy is channeled into the attention they must give their child.

But sometimes a parent doesn't act protectively, and instead becomes even aggressive. Maybe it's because of an experience that they have had when younger—abuse, maltreatment, neglect, abandonment.

I believe that the ideal that God has created for us is protection, from a father. Unfortunately, we don't live in an ideal world. So, even though I admit to being surprised at my own father's tenderness, it is in the heart of God that all fathers should be instinctively like that.

THINK ABOUT THIS:

Maybe, like me, you are surprised by being shown compassion and tenderness. But it's what our Heavenly Father gives naturally. And super-naturally we can learn to receive it from Him, even when we may have never received it from an earthly parent. But it's a matter of being open, of being able to accept His tenderness.

God's intention is to lead us to Him as He shows us His tenderness.

So often we can become weary and cold from the experiences of life. Cynicism can set in, overtaking our search for Truth. It can shadow our lives so that we can't see the sun or feel its warmth, or the love of Jesus—the Son!

God's intention is to lead us to Him as He shows us His tenderness. But we can use a 'de-fence', the fence of independence and unforgiveness to shut Him out, to make Him keep his distance from our hearts. We have 'locked the gate' of our hearts and we are now impervious to His love. We have 'thrown away the key' because we believe the lie that tells us that we have been too bad to be accepted by Him. Or, worse still, we believe the lie that tells us that His tenderness is not real, it's all a fairytale made up for the gullible few.

OVER TO YOU:

Can you accept the tenderness of God? I have often wanted to throw off His hand as He gently comforts, but when I can zero in on His words as I hear them softly in the distance and start to 'come to' from my unconscious (or unfeeling) state, I then can't ignore His call as He coaxes me gently into His presence.

God LOVES me and will CARE for me!

If you have 'locked up' your heart so that any compassion or kindness that surprises you is easier to ignore than to allow, then do yourself a favour and ask the Father to begin softening up the hardened ground of your heart.

Though we may be unused to the emotion of love demonstrated by care and compassion, the Truth in the Bible is that God actually loves us enough to care for us all the time. Let's allow the possibility into our minds and hearts: God LOVES me and will CARE for me!

Listen for His call amidst the 'stuff' that life deals out and the hardness that tries continually to knock us into an unconscious state rather than enliven us to abundant living!

Psalm 121

He will not let your foot slip –

He who watches over you will not slumber:

Indeed, he who watches over Israel will neither slumber nor sleep.

I love the words of the song "The Wisdom of Tenderness" by Crystal Lewis:

The wisdom of tenderness is
Accepting that I am his
Taking the fierce love he gives
And living it, living it.
Believing that I am beloved
Finding I'm free because of it
Unconditionally giving love is
The wisdom of tenderness.[2]

Father in Heaven,

The Truth of the Bible says you will not let me down. Yet life has often taught me to doubt this, and I find it hard to believe at times. Help my unbelief by lifting me today to a new and open place of faith in my heart and my mind. Amen

---

2   "The Wisdom of Tenderness" by Crystal Lewis.

4 Unfinished Masterpiece

A Progressive Work of Art

It was the Taj Mahal that had inspired dad so much. That a man could build such a monument to his love must stir a distant, God-given chord of creativity inside each one of us. A reflection of the character and heart of our own creator. The shrine that had become so famous in Agra, India, took shape on dad's piece of canvas that had been carefully selected and nailed to a weaving frame. It was to be a picture that would bring life, at the hands of an unlikely artist. As though he were creating his own musical composition, the 'notes' were stitched into the canvas—rising in volume and clarity as the image gradually formed. The Taj Mahal appeared discordant though to a young soldier, perhaps at odds with his present world. Yet in reality, what it represented was a memory of something so beautiful that it begged to be recorded.

Just like the builder of the real Taj Mahal in India, dad had begun a work that was to reveal something of his own heart.

Just like the builder of the real Taj Mahal in India, dad had begun a work that was to reveal something of his own heart. Beautifully woven threads were entwined artfully together. A textured piece, made of precious materials and possibilities, woven and stitched by a tortured soul that could turn and descend into the darkness of a colourless world in an instant. Turn over the tapestry and there lay a shock of tangled silk and cotton, jostling for position and seeking some sort of garbled order that belied the patterned and disciplined scene on its reverse. It was a reflection of his soul that was disheveled, disturbed, disappointed.

His creative juices flowed continually for a while, so that every spare moment was spent sewing the masterpiece. The threads and silks that he used were lovingly selected, bringing the artwork almost to life. Late at night he would sit in the lounge room, alone with the memories, adding a bit more to the legacy that needed to be left. The work provided a welcome respite from the pressures in his head. It softened the memory of war and calmed the whirlpool of emotion and injustice that threatened at each turn of life to drag him inward, spiraling toward a mire of choking mud—like the negativity that refused to release his mind.

On cold, blustery nights he would sit, just weaving threads in and out while the family lived around him. Alone with thoughts and memories, his heart would fly to the details of his tapestry, a welcome respite from the cold reality that he was living. A confusion of emotion and loss, injustice and abandonment reigned if he dug too deeply into the past few years. Better not to think too much, better just to take a long draw on the comforting cigarette that was constantly smoldering next to him in the battered ashtray. With a side glance he would put down the needle and silk thread and pick up the lighted stub, turning it on its end and grinding it into the aluminum ashtray with a force that made him feel better—at least for a while. Back to a lighter pursuit, back to the creativity that was his panacea, his salvation.

This world of colour and artistry satisfied a need to release the memories of India and all that he had lived through there. Quietly it would steal up on him: that haunting beat of drums, that unlikely combination of musical chords and notes played skillfully on sitar and tabla. And like a thin veil of organza curtain that could be pushed lightly aside to step into another room, he would enter the beckoning dimension that was his every time he lifted the needle and thread. Reliving all the fascination that he had often felt as a young soldier in that foreign, enigmatic world of the East, this rainbow work had become a retreat, a healing process, and an escape from the oft-remembered violence of war. Instead of the penetration of vivid nightmarish memories that clouded the mind, here was a gentle pastime that could refresh and renew the soul.

There was a stark difference in the extremes of behaviour in my father. On the one hand here was a creative person with an aesthetic sensitivity and a fine skill that showed in his artwork. But just as quickly the other side of his nature could present itself. He was weaving his own life, creating a picture of the person that he was. Strands of colour intertwined to tell a story, complete with all the twists and turns of a complicated piece of cloth that was both individual and masterfully created. Yet his frustration and his lack of patience would surface at a moment's notice, triggered by the smallest details, unraveling the threads of his current life that were so delicately but powerfully influenced by past experience.

I grew up to believe that I was perhaps responsible in some ways for his anger, and therefore that I could also behave in ways that could change him. If I saw a black cloud descend upon him, and could catch it early enough, I had myself convinced for years that I could make a difference. So naturally I would slip into a kind of co-operative state that I adapted to the situation as it presented itself. I lived much of my time in readiness to spring into rescue mode. Less a daughter, more a care-giver. If he were in full-blown anger mode, I would isolate myself from him. The tapestry of beauty on one side was all too soon in reality a tangled mess of emotion, if turned.

THINK ABOUT THIS:

We are each so much like a tapestry 'in progress'. Each of us is a work of art that is beautiful and complex. Often when life's circumstances cause us to 'turn' we can expose our 'tangled' side that's still being worked on. And often that's the side we don't want to present to the world, but would rather hide away. We don't like this 'turning', it's like a chaos that yells, "I'm unfinished!".

But the Heavenly Father wants to come and gently bring order to our lives when we are experiencing such disruption, both within and without.

Just like the discordant human nature in every one of us, there is beauty and there is darkness. He alone is the One who sees that in every one of us. No matter how we think we are unredeemable, past what anyone would ever want to rescue, he cares and sees us, and holds a mighty Hand out to bring us to safety.

The grace that we can know and operate in, as daughters of the Father in Heaven, is available freely to us. And that same grace can cover a multitude of an earthly father's shortcomings. We can forgive and have peace. We need to give that forgiveness out of grace, out of a heart that the Heavenly Father has given to us. That's what this grace is. That's what this grace inspires in those that receive it.

Our God is faithful to complete us—to make each of us the finished artwork of His mighty hand, so unlike my dad's Taj Mahal artwork that sits aging now, protected in a quiet cupboard. The tapestry is rarely brought out to the light.

This potential masterpiece of embroidery was never completed. I attempted it once, but now I know that as such, unfinished, it is a poignant reminder of the unfinished nature and character that is in all of us.

OVER TO YOU:

We often see the faults of others with perfect 'eyesight'. We judge them on the evidence of their behaviour towards us, whilst ignoring the need for change in ourselves. It's good to remember we are all a 'work in progress'. We are all a tangled mess in some part of our lives, and nobody has every single part of her (or his) life totally stitched up and looking grand from every angle.

Don't give up! I know that the Heavenly Father always brings His work to completion, unlike our human tendency to abandon and leave things undone.

Don't give up! I know that the Heavenly Father always brings His work to completion, unlike our human tendency to abandon and leave things undone.

Even if, for you, it is now too late for that relationship with an earthly father, it's never too late for the Heavenly Father to work on and in us, to finish and complete us in those areas that frustrate and anger; those parts of each of us that are exposed at the most inopportune times and are vulnerably open to the eyes of a critical world!

Philippians 1:6

"Being confident of this very thing, that He who has begun a good work in you will complete it until the day of Jesus Christ."

The words of a favourite hymn never fail to touch my heart:

Great is thy faithfulness
O God my Father
There is no shadow of turning with Thee
Thou changest not
Thy compassions they fail not
As Thou has been
Thou forever will be

Great is Thy faithfulness

Great is Thy faithfulness

Morning by morning new mercies I see

All I have needed Thy hand has provided

Great is Thy faithfulness

Lord unto me.

Father in Heaven,

Your faithfulness is really the ultimate. Thank you for never leaving or forsaking me, no matter whether I knew you were there or not. Help me to love and to forgive over and over again, as you have instructed us to do. And may I continue to work with your Spirit to be crafted into all that you have planned for me to be. Amen

Rocking Horse Romance

The Blessing of Generosity

With dappled grey, hardwood body and long, flowing mane, he stood in the corner of my room, upstairs in the little council house which was identical to rows of others in a neat English street. Ready to entertain me at a moment's notice, this most beautiful of rocking horses was a hand-me-down, but nonetheless my pride and joy.

Dark red reins draped his head, and he held a wry smile—as rocking horses do. His saddle was ever ready to take me to a new adventure. Though painted on, his beautiful eyes beckoned me with a life-like wink. Just a shake of his luxurious rope mane, and I believed in his whispering tales of new lands to conquer, new pastures to visit, long and rolling meadows to gallop together, with all my heart.

For many years I was too small to climb up on his saddle without help, but later as I grew I would spend time just rocking to and fro, thinking and dreaming little girl dreams. I was just the two of us, in our own special world. Coloured and faraway lands called me forth to play. They were lands of castles, princesses and high towers. Trusty steeds sped through thickly wooded forests, spiriting me away from lurking goblins and the like. For both terrors and true heroes lived in this magical world. And as we travelled through verdant glens and valleys, passing by imaginary friends, stopping in for tea parties at lavish estates with kings and queens, we would experience the adventures that only a child's mind can comprehend. He and I were one.

Coloured and faraway lands called me forth to play. They were lands of castles, princesses and high towers.

But as I grew up, my horse and I grew further apart. He was still mine, and still occupied that place of retreat in my room that offered dreams if I wanted them, but rarely then did I catch my dear friend's eye or hear his longing heart. Then he was gone. When I walked in and found him missing from his sunny spot in the corner one afternoon after a day at school, my heart sank. It's true: we tend not to pay attention to the precious things sometimes until they are no longer there.

Dad had actually given my rocking horse away! A friend of his at work, whose family could not afford a lovely horse like mine, had a little girl who needed him. So that's where he'd gone! My heart sank, and I sighed deeply at the thought of the end of my journeys to lands far away with people who lived only in my imagination. Strangely, though, I could sense a tiny feeling of curiosity creeping in through the grief, and waves of tears gave way to questions about the other little girl who now had become my horse's best friend. Would she care for him as I had? Would she love him and treat him well? Oh yes, countered my father, with an assurance and a confidence that secured again my shattered world.

As the weeks went by, my heart was captured by other distractions, and the rocking horse became a memory. After all, toys like that were for when you were little, and that was quickly becoming the past! Easter was always a very special time for me. For any child, of course, the thought of chocolate eggs and treats around that time is irresistible. But this particular time eclipsed them all. I so enjoyed the hymns of Easter. Every year as this festival came around and we gathered at our local Church of England at the end of the avenue, these hymns would lift me to a place that at other times seemed distant and foreign. Somehow they filled me with a joy, difficult to put into words, about Jesus. Happy songs, they inspired me and were filled me with life. My heart always seemed to feel Him when we sang them. After the Traditional Easter church service, we would take a walk in the country with Mum to the outskirts of our town, working up an appetite for a delicious English roast dinner.

But this particular Easter, expecting to arrive home to attack my *one* Easter egg from my parents, there on the kitchen table was the largest, most beautifully wrapped boxed *set* of Easter eggs I had ever seen! One enormous chocolate egg had been wrapped in red and silver paper with a stunning velvet bow across it, surrounded by dozens of smaller eggs all set in foil and coloured papers—a profusion of sumptuous treats to the eye that promised to be even more delicious to the senses when eaten. This exquisite box of chocolate delights was so large that it took up almost the entire tabletop. Oh, heaven! Dad was standing by, waiting to see my astonished little face when he told me that it was *for me*! And the reason? A thank you gift to bless us! It was from the little girl who now was enjoying my friend, my rocking horse, and my dear childhood companion.

THINK ABOUT THIS:

What does it take to reflect God's heart?
Generosity, care for others, and a vision to bless a neighbour. My father had taught me all three that very day.

The Perfect Father in Heaven is all about others. In fact, He was so concerned about all the others on Earth that He sent His Son down amongst them, to prove for them His love.

> **What does it take to reflect God's heart? Generosity, care for others, and a vision to bless a neighbour. My father had taught me all three that very day.**

When my dad showed that he was looking out for someone else's welfare, and that He cared about a family outside of us, he showed me a part of the Father's heart that I had never thought about. Now I was beginning to realize that the world did not necessarily revolve around me, but that others could benefit from what I had—from what I gave—and that there was always a reward of some description for kindness.

Thinking about people other than ourselves does not seem to come naturally to us as human beings. But we were actually designed by a loving Father to do just that. Does that feel foreign to you, in one of those quiet moments when we occasionally slip into being really honest with ourselves? Often it takes someone to show us the way in order to have us do for others what He commands us to in the Word of God, the Bible.

OVER TO YOU:

Generosity in many ways is so far from the 'natural me', but when I look around, I can find out the need of another. I can train myself to notice things and circumstances in which I can be a blessing rather than wanting to gather everything to myself.

Thank God that my father gave me the ability to think of others less fortunate. How would the world change if each of us daily asked the Heavenly Father to show us how we could make a difference for somebody in our world who would benefit from our generosity?

Psalm 112:5

"Good will come to him who is generous and lends freely. He has scattered abroad his gifts to the poor,"

Psalm 84:11

"The Lord God is my sun and Shield; the Lord bestows grace and favour and glory! No good thing will He withhold from me as I walk uprightly."

Father in Heaven,

Often I hug the hurts of life so very close that I can't see the lesson that you have in them for me. Help me to look up, look around, and to see what it is in each season of life that you want to teach me. Help me to understand that a generous heart is straight from you, and that even I can develop in that area. Amen.

6 Daddy's Tobacco Box

Pictures From A Wounded Past

It was one of those chilly, forlorn days of wind and wet, when the hearth is the coziest place—and tea and muffins dripping with honey are a dear and welcome treat! And as that evening closed in like a slowly gathering blanket, we began to experience one of the rare family moments that make the memories sweet, no matter how most of them turn out.

The Tobacco Box sat shrouded in mystery on a shelf in the lounge room cupboard, unopened by anyone except my father. With a narrow dent in the centre of its lid, and its emblem of sailor and pipe painted on a corner, its mystery fascinated me and called me to explore it! I can still remember its unique shape, colour and smell to this day. It was his special treasure. And it wasn't as if you could just ask to see what was inside! Oh no! You had to be *invited* into the world within this fascinating container. You see, it was the memorabilia of my Father's own cherished past, in the form of photographs—sepia, black and white, creased and 'dog eared' at the corner. A couple of home snaps had been 'touched up' by my father's own paintbrush, in an attempt to colour a world to look more real. On that sweet family evening all lay beckoning this child away to the past. To a world gone but never forgotten.

For a while there was a wistful quietness about his manner, as he gently held the precious memories and fondly but deliberately allowed himself to be persuaded to tell the stories of long ago. No sticky fingers allowed; the treasures had to be carefully handled. But then we listened intently as Dad told exciting stories of escape and intrigue, of army life and the War. But quickly something would rekindle a memory filled with pain, an episode a bit too deep, and the photographs would hastily be gathered from the gaze of a hostile world and bundled back into the box.

There it would sit again, alone on its shelf, shielded from the family and all enquirers, until Dad decided that it was safe to lift the curtain on the world of yesteryear for another glimpse. But perhaps not yet, for the pain still delayed its healing.

The Tobacco Box sat shrouded in mystery on a shelf in the lounge room cupboard, unopened by anyone except my father.

What was it that was so untouchable, so sensitive that we could never know about him? How to reach the heart of a man shrouded in the painful memories of time and tragedy? What is the path to the heart, the key to the emotions so deeply buried and locked with keys that since have rusted and long since gone missing? To me his history and heritage remained dimly sketched. I know that he was born into a family of opera singers, who traveled with a theatrical company in England; and that dad had resentfully been brought up 'in the wings'; theatre life being the norm, and his parents scant on family time.

Sent to boarding school whenever his parents toured abroad, burgeoning resentment drove him at 16 to enlist in the British Army. Many of the treasures in the tobacco box were photographs of Dad as a soldier in Kolkata, India. Dad playing the drums in the army band. Dad in the infantry, proud and fit in formation with his battalion, sporting one of the characteristic 'pith helmets' that epitomized colonial rule in India. Dad swimming in a tropical Indian lagoon. He told me once that he got so mad at the taunting of the other soldiers about his inability to swim, that one day he isolated himself from everyone and literally taught himself—such was the resolve and independent spirit of this teenage soldier. Now the tobacco box held photos of a military swim team that boasted much success, and in the front row, there he was, a champion!

But the God that I know could have helped my father to release the pain of his past, say goodbye to the open wound that continually troubled his soul. Perhaps, though the cure is there and the process is set in place, it takes a heart of openness and surrender; dad relied so much on his own will to resist, with the heart of one who fought so doggedly yet so alone. There was a sad melancholy, a faraway look in his eyes that I often saw. Having been forced to surrender at one time of his life to an enemy that treated him in ways that left the very obvious scars that he carried, I am convinced that he viewed surrender as a second and lesser choice in life. The fight against the past was the only way he knew.

THINK ABOUT THIS:

It's been said that "hurt people hurt people."

How true. When we don't deal with the breaking down of the hurt in our own lives, we become crippled and inward- focused, walking warily instead of in freedom.

We might love in part, but never with the liberty intended by the Giver of all love. We might relate to others, but perhaps we hold back the vulnerability that presents our hearts and surrenders our rights in order to enter into love with them. We keep a part of ourselves tightly shut up inside the 'box' that's a no-go zone, and we often deny ourselves the healing that is so readily available to us.

Pain can actually be an indicator that you have to dig a little deeper into yourself, a kind of 'X marks the spot' in the hunt for the treasure of your soul. Our Heavenly Father can bring us to a point of alliance with Him when we are no longer alone and fighting but strengthened and able. It's a place of unity with the Almighty, where hope and victory release us into a future of healing. That alliance can bring great freedom, but it has to be a choice to make that partnership!

Whatever the future holds, we hold our destiny inside us. It's held there like a tobacco box of treasures, ready to be released when we are ready to allow it. But sometimes the memories of the past that have shaped who we are now are too painful to just open up. And we find that we just can't move forward, can't lift the lid in order to allow the Father's Spirit inside where He could bring the healing touch that is so desperately needed.

OVER TO YOU:

The pain of the past, and its reminders, does not have to affect our daily lives right up to the present. We can surrender the pain of the past by speaking it out in prayer, no matter how much it hurts. God is not afraid of our anger, frustration and pain. He is not upset at our honesty! If you have delicate and painful things inside, start to talk to your Heavenly Father about them. Healing comes from our surrender. Our partnership or alliance with the Holy Spirit *will bring change.*

The pain of the past, and its reminders, does not have to affect our daily lives right up to the present.

Psalm 147:3

'He heals my broken heart and binds up my wounds (curing my pains and sorrows)."

Psalm 46:1–3

"God is our refuge and strength,

Always ready to help in times of trouble. So we will not fear, even if earthquakes come

And the mountains crumble into the

Sea.

Let the oceans roar and foam.

Let the mountains tremble as the waters surge!"

Heavenly Father,

I need healing in my life! Because of my past or because of my future and the fear that it holds, I have held on to unforgiveness in me. Forgive my lack of trust and faith in you. I want to rely on and totally trust your Word. You say that you are there for me. Help me to open up the forbidden areas of my heart that keep captive my fears and to surrender them to your healing. Only then can I be confident that my future promises the best for me. Amen.

7 Granny's White Washed Cottage

Life Without Conflict

She was a diminutive lady, with a gentle Cornish brogue and cute brown horn-rimmed glasses perched on the end of her nose. She tended to be one of those old people who 'hold court' rather than endear themselves to you. She was one who resisted an offered embrace, stoical like a fortress. By that I mean that you 'approached' her rather than ran into her arms. You fought for and won her favour and her attention rather than being the instant 'apple of her eye'. An unusual person with an air of formality and in the eyes of a child, she was just scary!

My brother would imitate the way she ate her toast in the morning—nibbling rabbit-like and folding one arm across her chest as she held the morsel in the other hand. Her hawk-like eyes would search these cheeky grandchildren for some reason to discipline them and leave them quaking in a corner! She commanded respect but, when her back was safely turned, there rose in me an irresistible urge to giggle and to imitate her country ways. It was no wonder, in fact, that dad did not relish her company. His relationship with his mother-in-law was one that was distant, untrusting and quite cold, and his couple of trips to visit for the summer holidays had been only made out of obligation.

Granny had a little white-washed 'two-up-two-down' cottage, in the tiny north Cornwall village of Delabole. With picket fence and a fragrant country garden filled with lavender and adorned with colourful sweet pea vines laden with silken blossoms, her house was a delightful retreat from our town life in Gloucestershire. A hilly walk from the Atlantic surf-pounded beaches, the little village was the kind of place where everyone had a relative nearby and all knew one another by their first names. It was a place where the smell of fresh baked bread rolls from the local family-owned bakery permeated the crisp morning as you ran outside to play. Familiarity, far from breeding contempt, appeared to fuel a sweet and innocent atmosphere in the community, clean and fresh like the sea breeze that blew in from picturesque Tregardock.

In the village streets, cobbled paths and terracotta pots lazily soaked in both sun and rain. White, wooden sash windows completed the pretty cottages with a character all their own, and on spring and summer days caught the ocean breezes which would ruffle granny's floral printed curtains. At times those curtains needed to be anchored with ribbons to stop them flagging out of the upstairs windows like prisoners calling for rescue.

We would occupy the upstairs second bedroom of the little house. The memory of freshly-cooked Cornish mussels in vinegar, washed down with Somerset cider or ginger beer has remained with me from the early years. It was always the supper-of-choice that we would settle to after an exhausting day at the seaside!

Following a day at the beaches of Tintagel or Trebarwith, we would trudge home through buttercup-lined lanes and run between the country hedgerows speckled with spring wildflowers. Picking fern leaves to fan ourselves as we walked, we worked up quite a sweat, and it was a treat to round a corner and find the road finally was about to wind downwards, giving respite from the ever demanding hills. But the weather was unpredictable! Often we would find ourselves caught in a sudden downpour of English summer rain, and many times we arrived home to the white-washed cottage drenched to the skin.

Feather quilts adorned creaky, old-fashioned beds that were quite a job to reach up to when you were so little! Often Granny would make up a bed for me on the floor, consisting of beautiful down-filled quilts and knitted patchwork blankets. Falling asleep to the fragrance of fresh picked lavender sprigs was heaven! As the night time twitter of sparrows in the trees outside faded with the approaching sunset, all seemed well with the world and with me.

I can only remember one time that dad ever accompanied us on the annual trip to Cornwall. The problem of his lack of attendance, I think, lay in his approval rating with Granny! She had an opinion of him that pretty much sized him up as not *quite* good enough for her daughter. There was not much that brought a word of approval from the old lady, and Dad was not into the game of striving for it.

Many a year we had such wonderful memories to paste into scrapbooks and reminisce over in the future. But most of those memories were without dad. It was a carefree holiday, every year. We could forget the strife and the arguments of every day at home. There was little tension in the air when mum was without dad. And yet they would write love letters to one another when apart. I remember sneaking a quick look at one that dad had posted that summer. It was an insight into his fondness for Kathleen, his wife, my mother:*"do you still have a crush on me, my darling?"* Quickly I closed the letter and threw it back onto the bed where Mum was sleeping. But I could not get the words out of my head.

THINK ABOUT THIS:

Peace and harmony need to live in every family. Yet some of the time it's an opposite spirit that operates! It's hard to live in peace, and it often takes us removing ourselves to another place to experience it.

When I settled into that feather bed of Granny's, I could almost feel the peace wash over me. It was a place of retreat in the midst of her stern nature and ordered ways. The places of retreat and peace in our lives

The places of retreat and peace in our lives are the places we need to visit often.

are the places we need to visit often. Even when we have suffered and can remember that life has not treated us well, it's up to us to seek the place of peace that will feed our souls, to retreat to fields of tranquillity that await as we release all that we are.

And at that place, we connect with Him who knows us so very well.

God is a god of peace in families. He wants us to dwell each day in good relationship with others. Not only when hearts are fondly remembering, but every day when the cares and trials of life abound.

OVER TO YOU:

We have to allow ourselves to just be 'real', in a quiet place. Do you have a place that is peaceful that you can go?

Busy lives and a frantic pace can cover up for a while, but eventually we all need to actively find rest and replenishment.

God is the one who is able to put back together the shattered pieces of broken daughters, in that place of rest.

I Peter 1:2

> May you have more and more of God's special favour and wonderful peace.

Psalm 46:10

> Be still and know that I am God.

Father in Heaven,

It's a fact that often peace can evade me. I know that, because life gets me down and I feel 'less' than I know that I can be! Help me, Lord, to find that place of peace and assurance. That rest and replenishing that comes only from a relationship with a divine heavenly Dad. Help me to rest and just be 'me'… as you created me to be. Amen

The Country Road

Enjoying The Ride

Hunched over the handlebars, he cradled to his chest his young daughter, the wind catching her dark hair and blowing it every which way, like the spirit of her unguarded heart. That heart would soar with untapped dreams of the future, hopes and desires that had yet to be even put into words.

My dad, with his flying cap and large dark goggles, cut a comical figure as he drove the motorbike and sidecar along country roads, determined to give his little family a new experience! The machine was the pride and joy of his life, and Sunday afternoons were just a treat driving through the countryside, checking out the side roads and lanes overgrown with wild flowers and sweet smelling vines. Another crooked lane, another bump in the road, but we always seemed to arrive in one piece. Reading this, you would think that maybe it was a cute car or little sporty number that we rode in as a family, but no, this was something that would now be a museum piece, a mode of transport plucked right out of the movies, romantic and liberating to all who rode in her!

The pillion seat was the chosen place for my brother, who would hang on for dear life to dad's jacket. Dad had a pillow tied onto the fuel tank of the motorcycle, and I would be perched precariously on it, leaning into his chest. Mum and Rover (the family spaniel/retriever who was no less a child, though canine) squashed up together in the little sidecar made for one. Truly cozy! Over the hills and valleys we would travel, caring not for the safe life! And always the trusty thermos flask filled to the brim with hot tea, the freshly baked Cornish pasties wrapped in towels to keep them warm, complete in a daintily packed basket, wedged in the corner away from Rover's sensitive nose! Across the county we would drive, past patchwork fields which were dotted with colour-drenched wild flowers spread across their hills, as though they had been painted by numbers and punctuated with little copses of trees. We had very few concerns and worries on those days. Only the anticipation of an exciting world yet to be discovered that would remain inside a memory in a little girl's heart.

This was a world in which daddy's arms were strong and protective, his sense of direction and safety the trusted and dependable constant of her life.

This was a world in which daddy's arms were strong and protective, his sense of direction and safety the trusted and dependable constant of her life. These kinds of days erased the memory of angry words and emotions, which charged like black storm-filled clouds and hovered on the horizon of her life. What delights waited for Harry Stokes and his little family on one of these rare but happy outings? Mostly I don't even remember what happened when we got there, but I do so remember the *journey*.

I recall the feeling of being held in strong and capable, caring arms. There is nothing that can replace the arms of a father. And yet it is the stuff of childhood and of dreams. But the need of a daughter for her daddy is true in both senses, that of both the earthly and heavenly fathers. I've wished often that I could have stayed inside the fantasy of being the little girl with a daddy to look up to, as many of us have. But another reality hits us as we travel the journey of life in this stark world. The reality is that daddy is never perfect! He is not able to fulfill every dream. He is not always there with the sought after embrace, the soft words for his daughter. And this reality is sometimes hard for us.

THINK ABOUT THIS:

Would we rather live in a fantasy world that brings feelings of comfort and sweetness than face loss and pain and stark reality of what really exists? We can feel like we have lost something precious as life progresses, and indeed we have. Like a gossamer silk scarf whipped away by the wind that gusts and whips around your face, so is the stealing of a memory of the precious and memorable moments of our lives by time. Reaching out to catch it, you may cry at the emptiness that it leaves as it fades to a distant and misty memory.

It's hard to put your finger on what it actually is that has been lost:

sometimes there's just a sad emptiness and regret at not being able to feel the way you once did, a memory that continues to evade recapture. But recapturing the good in the memory is something that we can benefit from doing.

This is what is important—to ensure that we arrive having experienced happiness, joy and good company.

OVER TO YOU:

In order to do this, we may have to recall the good and precious things that have gone before, majoring on the positive effect of that precious relationship with a father. Perhaps the journey *itself* is the priority. Perhaps when we need to face the world of today, we can soften it with the memories of the caring, strong arms of a daddy who loved us here?

And if not, if there is a memory only of sad and empty relationship when it came to a father, perhaps we can recall a time when the Heavenly Father was watching us as we suffered, because one thing I do know: He was there. He was ever present. His heart was never detached from

His immense love and compassion never left us no matter what we went through. His strong, caring arms were never far from us.

us. **His immense love and compassion never left us no matter what we went through. His strong, caring arms were never far from us.**

Psalm 84:11

> For the Lord God is a sun and shield; the Lord bestows favour and honour; no good thing does he withhold from those whose walk is blameless.

> O Lord almighty, blessed is the (daughter) who trusts in You.

Father in Heaven,

Help me to stop and remember those times when I was able to feel safe and protected as a child, those memories that energize and encourage me. Bring them to my mind in order that I may smile today and know that I have you, and all your strength and protection, love and joy, to bring me a hope for my future. Amen

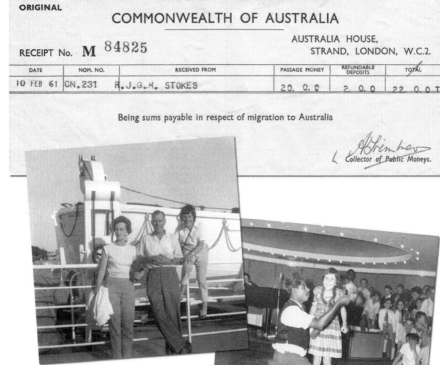

L to R: Dad's great smile! The Oriana en route to Australia, Receipt of total paid for our fare England to Australia, Mum, Dad and Valery on board the ship, Valery and the Cobra!

Section 2

THE JOURNEY

The war was finished and families were settling into a much longed-for peaceful existence. It seemed everyone had participated in some way towards the war effort in the country. Conversations often referred back to the days when the British people, through camaraderie and a 'stiff upper lip', rallied together as one.

But discontent was stirring. Men and women who had bravely and self-lessly fought a war that had changed everyone's lives now started to choose a new path for themselves and their young families. They began to look further afield for a new challenge. The small island nation of Great Britain started to give up its ex- soldiers and those whose spirits were restless within them. Emigration began to be an alternative for those who wanted 'more' for their children. And so the movement began.

It was in the late 1940's and early 1950's that both Canada and Australia became the destination of choice for many who wanted a new life. But it wasn't until 1961 that my parents decided to travel across to the other side of the world and begin what was to become the dawning of a new era in our family. A journey to a new life.

9 Ship of Hope

Our Future in Hope's Hand

It was 1961, and, as we drove around the final corner of the road to Southampton docks, an enormous structure loomed before us, dominating the landscape. A great, white ship was anchored at the wharf. Craning my neck to be able to see to the very top of the structure, I shaded my eyes from the unusual brilliance of the English sunshine. I could only glimpse in the distance far above us the cream chimneys that adorned the great ship's top decks, sending billows of grey smoke out into the blue, crisp April sky. Those clouds of dark smoke made their presence felt, but faded to a shadow like a charcoal drawing on smooth paper.

I tried to follow with my eyes some of the trails of the vessel's smoke as it spilled into the atmosphere; but eventually I needed to change my position, as my neck hurt! There was so much more to see though, and my enlarged eyes could never take in the massive excitement of the vista that was before me. What I had awaited for so long was becoming reality; and, like Alice in Wonderland, I felt completely immersed in a dream.

Gangplanks leaned precariously from land to vessel, spanning a gap from 'terra firma' to the adventure waiting beyond. Chattering excitedly, men, women and families were gathered in ordered lines awaiting their chance to board the great vessel. As the queue of people snaked slowly toward the great ship, the occasional runaway child would quickly be pursued by a harassed parent and returned to the line; for it was surely a parent's duty to rescue the runaway, but also a child's unstoppable need to 'break ranks' with unbridled excitement.

At the top many turned to take in a last long look at England: some with wistful gaze; others racing up that gangplank as though they couldn't wait to be aboard and at sea, captured by the thought of what awaited on the other side of the world! My mother, once atop the slightly swaying gangway, turned with moistened blue eyes and took in the scene, a slight wave reluctantly leaving her gloved hand as she noticed her cousin on the wharf flailing a lone handkerchief to get her attention. Perhaps the final look would be their last connection, who could know?

Months before we had set sail on our magnificent ship, I had intercepted the postman and taken that yellow envelope so filled with destiny to mum back at home, running full speed after having read the address and seen the initials OHMS clearly at the top. It could only have meant one thing—our sailing date to Australia! How excited and happy mum would be—this was what we had been eagerly awaiting for months now—and, here it was! It seemed to me that dreams actually do come true, and that what you wait for in the future, will surely eventually come to pass. We had talked about the trip so much that it was all I could think about, all that I would chatter to dad about in quiet moments!

The little girl of nine could hardly believe that the actual ship that was to take us all to far away Australia was now here—and surely it was a skyscraper! As we set foot onto the ship itself, I was convinced that this was just another building, except that I had seen the water, way down below, as we slowly travelled up the wooden and rope gangway on our approach to *Oriana*. About to start only her second journey ever, the ship was magnificent! Everything had its own special fragrance or look—nothing tarnished, nothing bent or crooked or wanting in any way. Just like the dream! Together our little family had awaited and envisioned this journey—across to the other side of the world—to our bright and promising new future. My brother and I would 'eat our way down the menu' at dinner time. I quickly developed a penchant for tomato juice—and silver service! Playing the princess felt like it came, well, naturally! From the fun of swimming pools to a movie theatre, plus programs for kids which meant daily entertainment, we were in for a heavenly journey!

The captain of *Oriana* gave three mighty bursts on the ship's horn, and she belched out puffs of smoke as if to wave goodbye to England. Signaling our departure, the enormous vessel quickly moved away from the wharf. Too late now to change our minds. Too late to return. It was now onward and eastward. The future awaited us. I stood next to dad on 'A' Deck, grabbing the railing as he held mum's hand tightly. Tears trickled down her smiling face, and I wondered that adults could be so complicated! Nobody spoke, though the noise of so many hearts rifling through mixed emotions was almost tangible.

Filled with hope and joy about the future, destiny beckoned my child's heart. I was yet unstained by the cynicism of the years. I was still untouched by the difference between expectation and reality. It was to be a life in a new country where the history was short, the culture was strange and the future uncertain. But hope still filled me to the brim with a bright new tomorrow, never mind what the past had held.

THINK ABOUT THIS:

So very often we pass HOPE by, and retreat into a well worn pattern of negative thinking that can make us limp through life, when we should be flying. Perhaps hope takes more energy, more forward thinking, than to settle into the 'status quo' of our minds. That's such a comfortable place to live! But we are called, as human beings who are growing

Hope springs readily from the human spirit if given the opportunity.

and being transformed daily, to address the negative areas of our minds, to move forward, to heed God's prompting in order to become more like Him!

Hope springs readily from the human spirit if given the opportunity. Particularly in the life of a child, it is ever ready under the surface to blossom and colour any life that cares to take hold of it. Hope is the heart traveling into uncharted territory much of the time, into unknown oceans where brave explorers dare to go to bring home new and exciting treasures to furnish their houses and to provide inspiration for a generation to come and for those who have stayed behind in their comfort zones.

And memories can also play their part in Hope. Memories are ambrosia. Sweet and lovely to the taste, they disappear almost as soon as they have arrived. But they are always there, ready to be savoured whenever we dare to retreat into their tempting grasp. And they can indeed hold us, but it seems we can never really hold them.

And we can hold on to hope. There is a hope eternal that springs from a Father in Heaven who cares and watches over us. He is ready with a future that holds all the promise and excitement that a child can see as she looks towards her life's adventure. God brings the future to reality on the basis of our trust in Him.

Hope and trust go together. They work in partnership as they guide us in a positive way.

OVER TO YOU:

We may have had our 'hope' dashed into splinters that fly away with the wind from one of life's storms. But if we have left our hope, and are now experiencing hopelessness, it's time to take hold of the future with an expectation of Biblical hope; that is, a confident expectation of a future happy end.Hope can again 'spring eternal', and it is time to turn your mind away from the 'comfortable' and start to take hold of the 'eternal' things which concern us all. It will be a challenge, but worth it! Exercise your trust in Him today, small steps at first, then bigger, until trusting is no longer hard for you.

Jeremiah 29:11

I know the plans I have for you, declares the Lord, plans to prosper you and not to harm you, plans to give you hope and a future.

Luke 18:17

Anyone who will not receive the kingdom of God like a little child will never enter it.

Proverbs 13:12

Hope deferred makes the heart sick, but when my desire is fulfilled, it is a tree of life

Heavenly Father,

I realize that sometimes it's very hard to hope about my future because it's the unknown. But you know about it already, because you are already there—in my future! Help me to trust and to rely on you at all times and through all circumstances, knowing that you are in Heaven loving me through every moment! This is called faith, and I need it. Amen

10 Dancing with Daddy

The Romance of The Dance

As we stepped onto the floor, my heart was swept up by the lilting music. It moved my young spirit and made my feet want to dance. He cradled my hand in his and we were away, pulled into the rhythm of the song, like being carried along by a gentle wave in the ocean on the sunniest of summer days.

The Grand Ballroom, decked out for a fine evening of entertainment, was resplendent with colour and romantic atmosphere. On our arrival the room had caught us with its magnificence as my daddy and I stepped, arm in arm, across the threshold. We had entered into another world—one of music, laughter and the magic that is created by those intent on the enjoyment of the moment. Stooping down just a little, he had turned to me and asked, "Shall we dance?"

And as we did, the scene unfolded. I was enthralled as elegant waiters floated past, balancing thin-stemmed wineglasses filled with pink champagne on fine, silver platters. Graceful ladies in full dresses with tulle petticoats laughed over wide-glassed, fruit garnished cocktails, seeming for all the world like they were royalty enjoying an evening out on the town. Colours blended, swirling gently into one as they swayed to the ebb and flow of the orchestra's music. Cares were swept away and laughter drifted on the night air. As we passed each table we would hear the comments by people enchanted by the scene of father and daughter sharing a lovely chapter of their lives together.

Pretty tables, daintily set and sporting stiffly starched white tablecloths, graced the edges of a polished dance floor. In a moment my child-wide eyes had taken it all in, and the decision was made. I decided that this was to be a wonderful night! I danced with the person in my life that had been given the role of courageous protector, shield and provider, nurturer and authority. In my newest red party dress I felt as beautiful as the heir to the throne of a fairy-tale kingdom somewhere in Europe, as blessed as a princess who had stepped into her own birthday celebrations with a specially selected guest list. And now the dancing was beginning!

Twirling me around, masterfully guiding my steps across the floor, my little frame dwarfed in his big arms he whispered dancing instructions—one, two, three, one, two three—humming the tune and occasionally breaking into a soft whistle. Encouraging me in my faltering attempts to keep up with his well-timed steps, his soft, loving words, "that's it, you've got it now, that's the way," released in me the confidence to keep going, keep dancing, keep enjoying this graceful journey across the floor. I struggled to master the steps, to keep up with his larger stride, but as he led me gently through the 'quick, quick, slow' beat in time with the music, I felt myself start to relax and enjoy this most amazing moment. It was easy when you had a good teacher! When I stepped on his shoes as I nervously followed him, he smiled and looked down, and confidently continued to lead me through the experience. My hand was locked in his, my heart singing to the music.

My hand was locked in his, my heart singing to the music.

Yes, I remember the magic of that night. And I smile. I didn't think of dad that way very often—courageous, nurturing, a provider and a protector. My heart remembers a wonderful night shared in the dance, but reality recalls that we did not share that great friendship all the time. The truth is, I remember this night so very fondly because it was so different. There were no harsh words, no disagreements, no frowns, scowls or negativity—just a fun, wonderful memory. A little girl and her Prince called Daddy.

As I grew older I began to realize that dad's character was not perfect, even though as a little girl I expected it to be! Many of his attributes, his attitudes and the differing facets of his life have left me feeling let down, abandoned and alone. I understand now that there is no perfect father here on the Earth, and, as wonderful as our impression of our Dad is, perfection is actually on the other side of Heaven itself.

THINK ABOUT THIS:

In my life I have come to believe that my father was the one responsible for shaping a lot about me. But he could only do that to the extent of his own worldview and ability. If only my picture of dad could have stayed as it was on this night! Because every daughter is born of an earthly father, she has a concept in her mind of how fatherhood looks. Depending on her human experience, no matter how hard she may try to visualise God, unless there is a supernatural overhaul of this mind's image, she will perceive the Heavenly Father inside the parameters of her earthly experience and history.

Daughters may in vain wait for their earthly fathers to relate better, to act differently, to reassure and encourage them more. But many men will never be the kind of father that a daughter longs to know. So we as daughters are often left with a feeling of being incomplete. We are left with a feeling of having no role model of fatherhood that we are content with. There remains then a need to reach out and try to make our father someone that they never were, are not now or ever could be.

For me, I constantly battle with the image from my childhood of the distant, mostly stern and sometimes anger-filled man who loved me. Memories that I have of him colour a lot of my natural reactions, are part of who I am. But without the supernatural influence of my Divine Father, that paternal image builds for me my image of God Himself. We have no image of this Heavenly Father to speak of in our mind's eye. Perhaps a dramatisation or a film memory of how Jesus is portrayed forms our picture of who this Person is. Most people, though, build an image of God upon who their own earthly father was in their lives. That is, until they really get to know this God.

This Heavenly Dad that I eventually met and got to know, and am continuing to find out about, taught me so much more about myself and my relationships. Our image of our earthly father is often tainted by his human faults, which leaves an imperfect memory. Often we will wipe out that memory because it's painful.

OVER TO YOU:

We form our picture of our Heavenly Father in a similar way to the way we see our earthly father. But this doesn't have to be the way we see God. We can learn to see Him as He really is.

How? Understand that humanity is frail and fallen, and then it's easier to come to terms with our earthly father's shortcomings. Understand that the Truth as laid out for us in the Bible describes God as He really is, and then we see that God doesn't have shortcomings. He is perfect, yet readily available to us. So now we don't need to see God in the light of who daddy was or is. We don't need to 'judge' our Heavenly Daddy with any measure that we have used for an earthly man.

Is there a memory that might need healing from you and your father's relationship? Bring it before the Father who loves you dearly and wants to comfort you in pain.

Is there a memory that might need healing from you and your father's relationship? Bring it before the Father who loves you dearly and wants to comfort you in pain. It may be hard to do, but beginning this way will start a whole new trust in Him—and healing for you. The Father in the Heavens wants to 'dance' with you!

II Corinthians 6:18

I will be a Father to you.

And you shall be My sons and daughters,

Says the Lord Almighty

Ecclesiastes 3:4

A time to weep and a time to laugh,

A time to mourn and a time to dance.

Psalm 30:11

You have turned my mourning into joyful dancing.

Father in Heaven,

I want to dance with You an eternal dance that lifts me and inspires me every day. Help me to understand that you are my Eternal Father and that you are always good and generous of heart to your children. Amen.

Cobra!

Confidence In His Care

The crowd circled around me, and I heard those nearest catch their breath as one. Out of the corner of my eye I noticed the swift movement of a lady as she stifled an anxious cry, cupping her hand over her mouth, her eyes growing wide with shock.

The snake wound itself around the warmth of my neck and settled in quite comfortably.

Cringing, I drew my shoulders up, trying hard to smile a little as the ship's photographer snapped a flash and caught the moment on film. The snake wound itself around the warmth of my neck and settled in quite comfortably. This Cobra had smooth, kind of wet skin, and the heaviness of its body weighed me down.

It was hard to relax into the experience, as the trainer was trying to tell me to do in his broken English. He waved his hand towards me, indicating to the people who watched in disbelief that I was a willing and able participant in his stunt. My lack of confidence in his words was evident. But I had a trust and no fear. My daddy was watching and looking after me. There was no doubt at all in my own mind that things were fine. This was amazing! The scales and the slinky, sculptured head under the control of a skilled trainer. Oh! That tongue whipped in and out so quickly it made me jump—sometimes coming way too close! I moved my neck slightly to the side, as if that would make a difference to its range.

I shivered a little but obediently complied with the instructions I was being given. Though people around me were encouraging me and whispering about my bravery and courage, I honestly could not understand what all the fuss was about. You see, my dad had already told me that, "They milk the snake's venom before they bring them aboard the ship!" While my heart beat wildly in my chest, and my face grew pale and strained, I put my trust in this man who knew all about snakes, among many other subjects—because, after all, he *knew every-thing about everything!* He was my dad.

We were in the Middle East, and, as we sailed our way towards a new life and a new land, we stopped at foreign ports that would bring new experiences and new revelation about the strange and wonderful world around us. It was in the days when the Suez Canal was a thoroughfare to the southern oceans of the World. The exotic surroundings and atmosphere, of a culture so very foreign to the European one that we had left, highlighted the very nature of the change that we were making to our lives.

Often, Dad would be the one who would introduce us to the new experiences, helping us to brave the unknown in order to learn and to grow. Comfortable and knowledgeable about the culture of this strange part of the World, this was now his territory. His joy showed as he confidently introduced us to savouring the pleasures of the unusual, inviting every strange nuance of foreign culture into our existence and our experience. Whenever I look at that photograph now, I wonder at the naïveté of the little girl in the picture. Her youth and her tiny frame seem to be encompassed by a natural enemy at close quarters. And yet in the midst of fear there lingers a childish trust in her eyes, an impish grin that belies the circumstances of the scene at hand. No sense of terror as she smiles for the camera.

Often, no matter what type of danger threatened, no matter what imminent tragedy loomed, daddy was there to protect, calm and guide. Through all the damaged emotions and the scars of the past, he was able to love and to care just like any natural father has the ability to do. There were times like these when he was truly the most wonderful man in the world to me. There was an easy confidence in what my father said. In those younger years of mine, it was always the truth and always to be taken for granted as being *the* answer. But as I grew to observe his faults, his failings and his own lack of confidence at times, I started to realise that the words that came from his mouth would not always be right, often proving to not always be truth.

In fact, he did not know everything. Long after our voyage to Australia from England, the revelations of an imperfect father began. As I became older, I started to realise that I could out-talk and out-argue him in many things! But I would never push it too far, never cross the line, in case there would come that black cloud of anger, that old familiar crossover into disapproval. And so I danced on the line for most of my teenage years. I danced a delicate balance in conversation, never sharing my true heart with him; for fear that it would be too much. A tipping of the scales into the mouth of the snake. And perhaps the cobra would hiss and turn on me. And perhaps its venom would be real. It was easier now just to keep my distance. Not to share my heart, not to bare my soul. A distance developed, a gap between two hearts that would never be really reunited.

THINK ABOUT THIS:

Our behaviour in relationships is so often a product of what we have learnt as children, or in growing up. I sometimes wistfully think of the times when my heart was so open and so trusting. Now it's really a battle to become vulnerable, to be a child of trust. You know, if we can just uncover and bring into the Light those words, those situations in which we have allowed lack of trust to take a hold, then we can indeed uncover the child-like faith and trust in a loving Heavenly Father that eludes us much of the time.

But the python-like grip of the past, whether it be memories of abuse, or mistrust or situations where we cannot forgive those closest to us, will always have us in its grasp and never quite out of its reach. That is, of course, unless we determine to break free and stay free. And freedom comes at a cost. But freedom, though it cost us, is not far from any one of us at any time. The love and acceptance of the Heavenly Father is never far away. He is waiting for us to discover His words, His open heart for us, His love for us. But much of the time, we refuse to surrender or listen to His prompting, due to our own superficial 'experience'. We let the exchanges and incidents of the past dictate the reactions of the now and the habits of the future.

Relationships can be strained enough, and when we allow the baggage of the past to be carried into them, we often find that we are misunderstood by others. Our quick and defensive words, our attitude of self-protection are often misconstrued as people receive us and relate to us on 'face value'. They don't have the history that we do, or carry the hurt of past situations. How can they understand what makes us feel and react this way?

And we're held in a grip. The 'grip' binds us from within. This python that squeezes life and love from us, is often not as obvious as a reptile entwined in our hair, clutching us to disable our limbs. No, the grip of that more subtle creature is unobtrusive and tightens with every advancing year. It is the grip of unforgiveness that squeezes the life out of us, quietly stifling our screams for help on the inside. It is the grip of abandonment, and the tight clutch of 'lack'. It's a gripping lack of self worth, a lack of validity, a lack of value. This lack is the opposite of what the Heavenly Father wants for us. And far from allowing us to grow, it stunts our every move toward love and health in life. Because it constricts our growth, and ties us up, it denies us the freedom to live in relationship with the Truth. If only the snake would loosen its hold. If only the python would drop to the ground and allow us to walk in freedom!

But, you see, we have not been told that this 'python' has already been 'milked' of its venom! See! All it takes is a confidence and a Word from Him to reassure us. He knows everything! His heart is for you. No need now to remain in the grip of that stranglehold that has been carried through life because of our ignorance of the Father's love and forgiveness! No need to live in the state of heart and mind of forgone years. No need to carry on the poison that has already been made void!

OVER TO YOU:

A lack of confidence acts like a stronghold around a heart; it's a constriction that can be loosed, and must be, in order to be able to breathe in the life that we deserve. Confidence comes from knowing the Truth—and that comes from the

Confidence comes from knowing the Truth—and that comes from the Father's Word. It is literally the Truth that sets us free!

Father's Word. It is literally the Truth that sets us free!

Let's not look always at our circumstances, but look to what God says in His Word about our future and us! Trust AND make a *deliberate* step forwards to believe that we can be confident in Gods nearness and favour at all times. What might that step be for you?

_____

Jeremiah 17:7

> But blessed are those who trust in the Lord and have made the Lord their hope and confidence

Proverbs 4:22

> Pay attention, my child, to what I say. Listen carefully. Don't lose sight of my words. Let them penetrate deep within your heart, for they bring life and radiant health to anyone who discovers their meaning.

Jeremiah 29:11

> For I know the plans I have for you says the Lord. They are plans for good and not for disaster, to give you a future and a hope

Father in Heaven,

Help me to be aware of the greatness of your care and concern for me, and your unfailing power to love me and bless me in my life. You are for me and not against me! Enlarge my confidence in you through your Word in me, I pray. Amen

The Italian Café

An Excursion to Joy

It was a magnificent Mediterranean morning. Spring approached and found us on board our ocean liner, swiftly cutting through the aqua waters of the ancient harbour of the Bay of Naples. The ship's elegant proportions belied her size, as she quietly drew alongside the wharf. Its crew and passengers we were about to be transported into another world.

This was Italy. The unfamiliar sound of its language was a fascination to me, and I longed to sound out those musical syllables—but I could understand not a word! That wonderful language, my first impressions of the country, resonated in my mind like a persistent but incomplete song—colouring my anticipation of lands yet to come. Italy affected me like music I couldn't get out of my head. I suddenly felt the excitement rising within me that only travel and new experiences brings. The people spoke a romantic, lilting tongue with mind-blowing rapidity, waving expressive hands at one another and drawing this onlooker into their world with entrancing gestures. I felt a part of them already, and our excursion had hardly even begun!

Dad caught my nine year old hand as we walked down the gangplank together onto dry land, gathering our thoughts and our family, and deciding which way to wander, shop, and taste the delights that this new city had to offer. Shop keepers welcomed us in the local Italian dialect and beckoned us to sample their goods and delicious foods. Their smiles and banter drew us into one establishment after another, up and down little winding streets, as we sifted through tiny village squares forgotten by time.

Clutching one another's hands in order to cross the road in one piece, we soon realised that everything in Naples brought a new experience. Not the least of these was the colourful nature of the people and their personalities, particularly when it came to driving! The traffic appeared to be chaotic, with no enforcing of road rules or respect for another's right to share the road! Intersections became a dangerous game of 'dodgem cars' as little Fiats and other European cars vied for position and advantage, and near collisions became as commonplace as a squabble on a soccer field. There appeared to be no safe place for a pedestrian in the middle of this! Dark heads would appear quickly out of car windows as the commentary on the traffic, the day, and the driving skills of others who shared the road became the conversation, joined in by a jumble of the locals from the sidelines who crowded in to become a part of the game.

Dad steered his little family towards a small café with tiny tables and wrought-iron chairs which spilled out onto the street. Every table waved its red chequered cloth in the breeze, entreating each passer-by to settle into its vantage position to observe the passing parade! Each table-cloth was anchored only by cute bottles of olive oil and squat flasks of balsamic vinegar that crouched in pairs on the tables like rotund little Italian Nonas! The proprietor stood leaning against the doorway to the café. Laconically appreciating the mid morning sunshine, his big hands theatrically beckoned to all who would listen:

> **Every table waved its red chequered cloth in the breeze, entreating each passer-by to settle into its vantage position to observe the passing parade!**

"Come in, come in, you're welcome…!"

This Neapolitan restaurateur was the picture of hospitality, the embodiment of his colourful and exciting culture.

Mum had donned a favourite outfit for such a beautiful day, and, as we negotiated our way through the crowds milling around the centre of Naples, she was indeed being appreciated by the local Italian men. Wolf whistles and the odd pinch on the bottom followed her little white shorts and unusual sandy coloured hair. She stood out amongst the locals, much to dad's chagrin, and he swiftly guided her, his arm firmly linked with hers, into a corner seat of the little café—away from those dark, prying eyes! Through the narrow and hilly streets of Naples we walked, sampling from each new stall and hawker at every bend in the road the delicious and tempting treats they each offered to those tourists from the big ship in the harbour.

Small groups of us wandered mesmerized by the sights and sounds of this Mediterranean culture so far removed from our own.

The sun was beating down with an uncomfortable heat as the day drew on. As it rose to its position high in the sky, it brought a strange new feeling—the freedom and adventure of travel and new places.

Dad did not speak Italian, but I was fast realizing that his love of languages meant that he could pick up and improvise an adequate communication with the local people in an instant. My admiration for this man widened, and I looked out from my position behind his legs with the enquiring eyes of a child, taking in the sights and smells of this delicious place and storing them in my memory for the future. As my father ordered a meal of spaghetti and octopus for me, my eyes widened, and my mind wondered how I would manage to eat such foreign delicacy!

By the time we had left the little café, stomachs full and spirits high, we had experienced the newness of yet another of life's pleasures. The shared experience of being foreigners in another land and partakers of a rich and exciting way of life that was a foretaste of what was planned for our future, would prove to be a uniting bond with one another to be recalled and relived when life's storms threatened to break down relationships between us.

Finally the shadows grew longer, and the day started to close. Hand in hand, we boarded again the big ship that waited in the harbour. A last glance back as the sun headed for the horizon, and we were safely aboard and ready for the next part of our adventure. Leaning over the banister on deck, as the big ship quietly and swiftly drew back from the dock, I took in the beautiful scene and breathed a deep sigh, inwardly promising myself to return to this romantic land. As twilight closed in, I could see the haunting shape of Mt Vesuvius in the distance. She dominated the horizon and brooded over the picture as though wanting to be remembered by every visitor. Silently she must have become etched in every young explorer's mind that day, influencing each child's thoughts of Italy whenever we would think of her in the future. I knew I would return one day to discover her secrets and strange culture. In future years, I would become fascinated by the history of the city of Pompeii that lay at the base of the volcano. Buried under tons of volcanic rock, it had been held prisoner with its people for many centuries—and I would not be satisfied until I returned to see it for myself. But now more of the unfolding journey awaited me, and Pompeii and the beautiful Vesuvius were for another day.

As a family, stored in our hearts were the deposits of shared memories, forged through experiences that would never be erased. They were to be enjoyed and drawn upon. Perhaps in another year, or even another decade. But always shared.

THINK ABOUT THIS:

It is sad that we can bury good experiences in forgotten memories. Only when one's senses are stirred can the scenes from long ago be revisited. Like the city of Pompeii lying hidden from the world for centuries, our memories are buried beneath the volcanic lava that has encased them and hidden them from our view and our remembrance.

Every experience is a part of every individual's own story. And the power of that story can be found in everyone's heart. Perhaps your story is not always positive, but often your experience can benefit others.

Often we neglect the power of family relationships. One of the things that I shared most beautifully with my dad was the ability to recall times of shared experiences. The bright, positive memories such as the day in

Naples are the ones that I like to focus on the most. They bring to mind the attributes of my earthly father which reflect those of my Heavenly Dad: protectiveness, a caring and guiding hand, and a voice that inspires confidence.

As I burrow into the memories, I can retrieve the treasures of long ago, and I can again enjoy the experiences, perhaps even the sounds and the music, of the life of long ago.

Each individual's story is not necessarily a 'testimony' to the truth about life. But our story can help others on the way, a guideline for those who need to hear it.

OVER TO YOU:

Each individual's story is not necessarily a 'testimony' to the truth about life. But our story can help others on the way, a guideline for those who need to hear it.

A testimony actually tells others that what you have experienced is valid and useful. In the case of your life experience, it's invaluable if it helps others to go forward, to have hope when hope may be failing.

So, tell your story, and also make it a testimony! Tell it with a 'positive spin' and remember that the dark times only serve to contrast with the shining moments, making them even more brilliant.

Philippians 4: (Msg)

Summing it all up, friends, I'd say you'll do best by filling your minds and meditating on things true, noble, reputable, authentic, compelling, gracious—the best, not the worst; the beautiful, not the ugly, things to praise, not things to curse. Put into practice what you learned from me, what you heard and saw and realized. Do that, and God, who makes everything work together, will work you into his most excellent harmonies.

Romans 8:28 (NIV)

Or that all things work together for good to those who love God, who; or that in all things God works together with those who love him to bring about what is good.

Father in Heaven,

Though some of my experiences in life have not been positive, I know that you have promised to work all things together for good for those who love You and are called by You. So I choose to focus on those good and lovely things that can be told in my story, as well as those things that are difficult to tell. Help me to help others with my story, as it becomes a true testimony to Your work in me. Amen.

Mistaken Identity

Who Do I Belong To, Daddy?

The sweat was running down my back. I had never before experienced this noise, these smells, this shock at seeing a culture so far removed from my own. The waves of heated air you could almost taste. Dirty ceiling fans thrashed above my head in every little shop we went into. I felt like pushing it all away, the living in it was too close, so very uncomfortable. Amidst the confusion and uncertain surroundings, I turned to grab my daddy's hand.

Amidst the confusion and uncertain surroundings, I turned to grab my daddy's hand.

In Aden the dusk of evening tends to descend very quickly, and soldiers had already started to put out rows and rows of little canvas beds for the hundreds of homeless people, many clothed in dirty, torn rags to sleep where they could. As I called to dad, he forged on ahead. Must have been the soldier in him—a re-living of perhaps the old life, as a British soldier on assignment in colonial India.

My dad had been the son of opera singers, born in the north of England. A 'Geordie', as he proudly claimed, a native of the Tyneside region of Northern England. But life growing up in the wings of a stage was not to be for him. Sing? He couldn't even hold a tune! So he was packed off to boarding school in order to give his parents the chance to travel with their opera company. The school holidays would often find him down working in the local coal mines, sent to 'earn a quid' for the family. So out of frustration at an early age, it was no wonder that he had run away from home and joined the British army.

Young Harry ended up serving over five years in the army as a private in peacetime, before World War II. Sent to India as a teenage soldier, he did his growing up and his maturing into manhood there, learning many of his adult skills in that peculiarly foreign land. Even though an insulated existence, it was, nonetheless, an adventure. With a wry smile he would recount the time that he had been bullied by the other soldiers because he couldn't swim. Taking himself off into the bush, he had found a suitable looking lagoon, where he had proceeded to spend a whole day learning to swim on his own! Such was the determination of the man, and the strength of his will to win, that before the end of his army career his swimming prowess was almost legendary.

Oblivious of me at these times of silent recollection and steeped in the daydreams of his yesterdays, dad would somehow become lost in a memory, in the strangeness of his time in India. Memories became a sudden assault on his senses. Pictures thrust themselves forcibly into his mind: scenes from long ago when he was a young man, comfortable with his life, confident in the strength of a much younger body and mind.

He was lost to us and distant from us at these times of recollection. That day in Aden with me walking beside him, he was paying me little attention. He absentmindedly grabbed the hand of a little girl who had been following us for some while. Unaware that the small hand in his was not his daughter's, he wandered on through the market place, relishing the sights and sounds, keenly experiencing the strangeness of this place so reminiscent of the culture of his India. This place had a strange and romantic familiarity, one that danced inside his mind to the music of long ago.

She was a frail little girl. Her hair was strung about her dark face and hung limply around boney shoulders. The scrap of a dress she was wearing had long ago lost its bright colour and now hung pitifully over her very thin body. A picture of neglect, she hung on to this big man's hand as though her life were depending on it, which indeed may have been the case. As she lightly stepped in time with him, she hoped that he would be her saviour and the one to redeem her situation. The only bright spot in her life each month or two, was the vain hope that a tourist would bless her with some monetary handout or word of praise, in the midst of her abandonment and life of rejection. No wonder she made a run for the hand of my father, and held on as long as she could. All of her hope, all of her future, had been apparently dashed long ago, and yet here was a glimmer of a bright beginning. But reality loomed for her, waiting to catch up with her, stealing the dream from her.

Turning at the sound of my voice, and quickly realizing his mistake, daddy dropped the little girl's tiny hand, much to her dismay and disgust! Her squeals of indignation and the expression of loss on her face would stay with us for a long time. The memory of that day and its case of mistaken identity would linger in our hearts, as a continual reminder of the contrast of our lives and hers.

I didn't give a lot of concerned thought to her as I grew up. I just moved onwards to the next part of the great adventure that I was living. What a different life I have had, what a world away from her I am now. What a distance is created by culture. That little girl in Aden had probably never known the hand of a father. She may never have known her worth in the Heavenly Father's eyes. Maybe she had never realized her potential on this Earth. Maybe she has died knowing only poverty and want. And here was I, able to slip my hand into the hand of a father and be taken out of that alien world, able to be removed far away from the type of life that demanded slavery, subservience and a resignation to hopelessness.

He was never one to speak about his achievements, preferring to keep it all quiet and let people find out. A photograph of the Army swimming team, bearing a mark above the head of one muscular young soldier in the foreground, bears witness to his dogged determination to win. Small tattered and brown photographs of tanned and muscular young men in army games and exercises spoke of a competitive spirit, a will to win. These photos were from my father's time in India, and this determined spirit would be the quality that would be his saving grace in the second World War years to come. Out of a childhood of want and near-poverty, he had made a life in a foreign land, turned around his fortunes that belied the beginnings of his struggling family ties. Though he still financially had little, he could see and remember days of long ago when children such as the little girl on the streets of

Aden surrounded him and his soldier mates, when the heat and the oppression of the third world contrasted with what was being held for him in his future. And he was headed for his future now, leaving the past behind—a world away.

THINK ABOUT THIS:

We can mistakenly believe that we are a product of our upbringing, and that our background limits us so we never achieve the potential that God has put inside the heart of every daughter. As I think of the little girl in Aden, I am often reminded about the grace of my Heavenly Daddy in all that He has given to me. Awakening my relationship with Him is the most amazing act of His supernatural grace.

In the midst of a life of confusion and spiritual poverty, this Heavenly Father grabbed my hand in the middle of a crowd and the noise and heat of life.

In the midst of a life of confusion and spiritual poverty, this Heavenly Father grabbed my hand in the middle of a crowd and the noise and heat of life. He transported me away from that life into His arms. He surrounded me with comfort, compassion and care. He fed me in the midst of famine, and favoured me with a life of blessing.

The sense of 'belonging' that we have when we are a part of a family is what gives us security. Often if we don't feel this, we will attempt to 'create' family in another way, through another context. It may be a 'surrogate' family that we wish we had been born into, or perhaps a bunch of people with similar interests to whom we can cling and feel a sense of familiarity and connection.

OVER TO YOU:

All of us have felt 'lost' at some time of our lives.

Maybe we've felt just like a little lost girl living on the streets of a country which is not our own. Perhaps you feel this way now. But knowing Jesus introduces us to a whole new, world-wide 'family' that cares and loves us. Suddenly we have inherited 'sisters and brothers' that we never even knew existed!

Today, let's begin to look around us and expect our Father in Heaven to show us those who are "daily being added" to our new family.

Psalm 68:5,6

> A father to the fatherless, a defender of widows, is God in his holy dwelling. God sets the lonely in families; he leads forth the prisoners with singing.

Song of Songs

> He has taken me to His banquet hall, and His banner over me is love.

Acts 2:46

> They worshiped together at the temple each day, met in homes for the Lord's Supper, and shared their meals with great joy and generosity—all the while praising God and enjoying the goodwill of all the people. And each day the Lord added to their fellowship those who were being saved.

Father in Heaven,

Though there are times when I may feel lost and alone, remind me always that you are near, that you have a family on earth in which you have placed me. Remind me that I am loved beyond words. Amen.

14 Traders in the East

Heart's Desire

Rising like a glowing ball from a straight lined horizon, the sun bathed its middle-eastern light on the scene, highlighting it as though a perfect stage were set and it had become the spotlight. Morning was breaking on the Suez Canal. The beckoning call of traders from way down below the ship echoed in the still morning air as we raced up the decks to see the bustle of what was going on out on the ocean.

In stifling heat and under a cloudless blue sky, we drank in the colourful picture that awaited us: tiny rowboats bobbing and weaving amongst each other; each boat vying for our attention and a position of advantage that would grant the owner priority in the eyes of their customers. These boat-bound shopkeepers eagerly and brazenly displayed dazzling coloured fabrics, cleverly woven garments and bright, carved leather bags.

I ducked and wove my way through the crowd as only a child can, trying to get a vantage point between the adults leaning over the rails. I could just see the boats with their wares below as I squeezed in between two people who were engaged in a loud bargaining with one of the sellers below. "Missy want lovely bag?"

They had so much to sell. But the owner of one of the boats caught my eye and quickly brought out his Piece de Resistance—a stuffed leather camel. It was big enough to sit on, complete with red saddle and an appealing but oddly coloured face—such a treasure! Now I was transported in my imagination to smooth-sanded yellow deserts, and the scene of a palm-treed oasis, where Bedouin traders acted out their roles of romance. The ancient trading rituals of the East compelled me, and I pleaded to be allowed to purchase this exotic prize. Oh how I wanted such a souvenir from the Middle East!

The romance of far-away places seemed to be distilled into this very moment.

Silken scarves from the local *souk*, purses to grace the arm, hand crafted wares that were almost irresistible to the romantic heart lurking below the surface of every little girl; this was irresistible!

What little princess had not lived in the fantasy world of Sinbad the Sailor, of Egyptian royalty and of sumptuous palaces filled with exotic riches to enjoy? Silken, skilfully sewn fabrics brushed subtly across your face as you passed through the ancient market, with attendants ready to provide for every whim of the young heart. So instantly I had been transported to another world, another life. The romance of far-away places seemed to be distilled into this very moment. The hope of a new life seemed to be funnelled here into this very time, as my formerly imagined pleasures and experiences grew into the living out of a childhood fantasy.

Captured as I was by the scene, I looked to dad for approval to buy an adorable handbag which had caught my eye. A nod of his head, and the deal was done. The seller tied it on to the end of a primitively strung rope, pulling it hand over hand up to where dad and I stood. Exchanging our money for the prize, the old man tipped his little hat in our direction, yelling, "You good man, good man, buy for daughter, yes?"

Years later, whenever I think of that little bag, if I concentrate very hard I can almost recall the atmosphere, the sounds, the feeling of total immersion in this foreign and exciting life. The smells, sights and rhythm of this portable water market will forever be in my mind's eye—probably because it was my first journey into such an ancient and exotic culture.

THINK ABOUT THIS:

Many times in my life my father showed me kindness and blessed me with gifts. Though the negative aspects of his personality would often intrude into the moment, there was generosity in his heart. But rarely would I realise that the gift was an expression of love. The action of giving was a demonstration of the care of a parent and a glimpse into the Heavenly Father's heart for every human being.

The action of giving was a demonstration of the care of a parent and a glimpse into the Heavenly Father's heart for every human being.

On this Earth I have felt many a time that I am exposed to a different 'culture' but am reminded that my family and I are 'just passing through', and that what awaits us is a homecoming to an Eternity filled with family!

There is comfort in knowing, though, that in the midst of a culture that tries to rip us off at times and tries to force us into living life in ways other than would bless the heart of God, we have a Father who cares, provides for us, and looks to our needs and hearts' desires—one who stands guard at heart's door, if we will let Him. That's the comfort that faith in a loving Heavenly Father brings.

OVER TO YOU:

Earthly dads can protect and comfort us, but we have the ultimate in Him who lives above this culture and life, who loves us beyond our understanding, and who wants to reward us 'Princesses' with the desires of our hearts!

If we really believe that our Heavenly Father gives gifts and wants the best for us, then why do we ignore them? Why do we second-guess His motives? Why do we refuse to believe in this aspect of His character altogether? The generosity of God is undoubtable when we look around us and start to think about His provision.

"I am not worthy of kindness, not good enough to be blessed". That may be the voice that you have heard from time to time. But it's not your Heavenly Father's voice.

Today, let's practice *reminding* ourselves of the grace and favour that we have in our lives. Remember that He pours blessing into our lives when we ask. Remember that each of His gifts is His expression of love towards us.

Psalm 13:5,6

> But I trust in your unfailing love;
>
> My heart rejoices in your salvation.
>
> I will sing to the Lord,
>
> For he has been good to me.

Psalm 85:11(b), 12

> No good thing will the Lord withhold
>
> From those who do what is right.
>
> O Lord Almighty,
>
> Happy are those who trust in you.

Father in Heaven,

Many times I tell myself that you wouldn't give to me as you give to others, because of who I am. But I forget that it's your nature to show generosity in every way to those whom you love, regardless of how I am receiving it. Help me to remember that your promises are for me, though I may not feel that they are. And thank you! Amen

L to R: Nissan Hut accommodation for families, Valery and two friends at a hostel birthday party, Valery and brother James at the door of their first Aussie home, Valery in the driver's seat of our first car in Australia, Floral tributes at the soldiers' memorial after dad's farewell

Section 3

THE NEW COUNTRY

Arriving on foreign shores was one thing when you were part of an army, but bringing your wife and two dependent children in one unit was quite another!

We are all on a journey to a new day. It's a journey that involves our ability to be constantly and consistently healed from the wounds of life's wars. It's a journey towards our dreams and desires, which often can seem unattainable. It's a journey that, when those dreams come to pass, is worth the ride.

And so the new life in this young nation of Australia began. Our hope was for a life of promise and prosperity; a life of freedom and wide-open spaces. A new life for an ex-soldier turned civilian and his family, adapting to a world that was not disciplined, regimented or in order....

Culture Shock!

Strange New Land

An early winter's morning mist swirled around the ship at its water line, embracing her as she quietly but powerfully cut through the Ocean's grey waters and made her magnificent presence felt in the harbour. Through a cold and oppressive winter drizzle, Melbourne docks loomed closer with every minute. We were about to leave the ship that had become our home for the past three weeks. This was what we had dreamed of—a new life, a new country, a new future!

As we disembarked into the waiting throng of officials and other new arrivals to this island nation of Australia, we joined what appeared to be interminable waiting lines, snaking customs and baggage inspection queues, making our way eventually to the bus that would take us forever away from the impressive ship behind us. *Oriana's* hull shone white and glorious in the now brightening Melbourne morning. The memory of it would always trigger for me some of the most beautiful times of my life. Those weeks had been the most wonderful, fun-packed adventures for both my brother and myself. But now we were facing the unknown and exciting future we had only dreamed about!

Like most of the children who had taken the voyage, we instantly put behind us the life that we had experienced until now, trusting it to our parents to take care of cherishing the memories, remembering the great times. It was for them to file away in their minds the adventures on the high seas till it was time drag out the stories and laugh and cry with those of perhaps a similar heart that we would meet some time up ahead.

Now it was time for the shipping company's ground crew to take over. As they boarded the grand lady and prepared to disembark her hundreds of passengers, I heard the characteristic Australian drawl for the first time. This new way of speaking, with its friendly laconic attitude, grabbed my attention straight away. I listened with eagerness to this foreign people. Fascinated, my heart was 'doing cartwheels' in my chest. Excitement reigned! These friendly people, with their characteristic drawl, always seemed to have a quick humorous quip at the ready like trigger-happy cowboys. The people of this new land spoke with kindness in their eyes and a smile at the corner of their mouths. And I mentally practised, as an intending new Australian, how I could sound more like them. The expressions were strange, though the words were the same. Their statements were made with, it appeared, a mere slight opening of the mouth. I liked them. This was going to be a great new life.

After being herded through customs and the necessary immigration processing, we boarded buses for many and varied destinations, bidding farewell to those families who were bound for a home on the opposite side of this great city.

And as we drove away from the Melbourne docks, we took a long last look at our ship and those other migrants who were yet to set their feet on this new land. They were yet to find their own piece of it and become a part of its culture; they were yet to feel the wisp of regret which was affecting me now, like the puff of white smoke escaping from the big ship's funnel, which, as it blended quickly into the southern sky, was like a final wave of a trusted friend.

So our little immigrant family became absorbed into this great land of Australia. Before long, we would be a part of this new society. Already we were adapting to the differing sights and smells of this exciting place. Like pioneers with a vision of destiny clearly in mind, we children looked forward to losing our "English-ness" by imitating the local drawl, as if practising a fresh language, and by planning time on the beach in order to sun-bake our whitened European complexions. Our bus bumped along the roads, and as our eyes took in the passing scenery we started to adjust to a different style of homes than those to which we were accustomed. These were red-bricked, single storey dwellings with driveways. This was so different from the tethered council houses of our old home, the semi-detached living that made separateness unfamiliar, and encouraged often a tight-knit and restrictive feeling. That was a place where driveways were unnecessary. It was a place where people had chosen to live small and cramped lives.

Here in this new place there were wide spaces, wooden telegraph poles with electrical cables strung listlessly between them, birds of unfamiliar song. We noted every strangeness to one another, as if wanting to remember it and bring the observation out later for a spin and some investigation. Eventually as we neared our destination, there appeared the odd shaped buildings of an old World War II storage area, now a hostel to house hundreds of immigrant families new to Australia. As they came into view, we peered through misted

We noted every strangeness to one another, as if wanting to remember it and bring the observation out later for a spin and some investigation.

windows and quizzically commented, wondering what we were now to encounter. Hope and enthusiasm for this new country brimmed in almost every heart as we anticipated eagerly what was before us. The future was an excitement waiting to be taken and savoured!

Clearing with my sleeve a small patch of the condensation, which now clouded the bus window, I felt the vehicle lurch into the hostel driveway. A group of children who had gathered on the pathway looked with curious eyes, checking out the latest load of newcomers to their domain. As we stepped off the bus I felt their gaze even more than the keen breeze and the misty rain that greeted us. But nothing could dampen my spirits as I braced myself for the next chapter of this, the most exciting adventure I had ever had.

There was a main compound of brick and wooden buildings, but what caught my eye almost immediately were the strange, half-circular huts that dotted the acreage. The whole area was enclosed by tall, wire fencing. Barbed wire topped the fences and was curled menacingly around each section. Dad explained that these huts were remnants of the War, and had been converted into living areas for migrants. I couldn't take my own eyes from the barbed wire and the feeling it brought of enclosure. Shaking off the creepiness of that, I looked ahead and realized that this was a temporary address, a sort of half-way house until we could become settled into our jobs, schools, and our new country. As the crowd of nervous new immigrants went through more official processing and were allocated their accommodation, we were issued with armfuls of sheets and towels, blankets and vouchers for our meals.

The central building housed an enormous canteen. There was to be no cooking in the huts, please! Strange laminated tables with chrome legs were regimentally set across a large, spacious dining room, which, though empty now, was at meal times occupied by mums, dads and kids thrust together by their circumstances and sharing a common goal, to make Australia a place that each could call home. During these meals we were to discover and meet many people who spoke differently, lived differently and thought differently! I began to practise a newfound skill of learning accents and language. As time went on I rapidly made new friends and became adept at mimicking the Scottish and Italian accents, often pretending that I was of a different background when outside the hostel. My friends came from everywhere in Europe, and together we made our new home an exciting mixture of old and new culture, a delicious melting pot that reflected the adult world in an Australia of the 1960's. Perhaps that's what made for a brilliant mix of rich culture that grew and forged a nation strong and unified, ready to apprehend a prosperity and richness in both its people and its future.

Government issue brown vinyl chairs at the end of long, linoleum-clad floors greeted us as we finally reached our very own hut. There were two bedrooms that contained bunks for us kids, and a main room with a convertible settee/double bed. Not much else really as we looked around and took it all in. Well, at least the boxes of our treasured possessions from England would fit in with plenty of room! (I was later to learn that it was a real step-up to be transferred from the Nissan Hut to a small brick ex-munitions storage building that had been basically renovated to house 'new Australians'. These were the pick of the accommodations at the hostel, which we eventually managed to secure after a year.)

Amongst it all, I could see the anti-climax of arrival was starting to affect mum. Having traveled from the other side of the globe, to come to a temporary home so uninviting and strange, was hard. She struggled to make this 'fun' for us, covering what disappointment she may have felt, and pointing out all the benefits of communal dining, having someone else to wash the bed-sheets instead of her and the fun of living with camp-style shared bathrooms!

I could see that it was the end of a chapter for dad. He was eager to find the place of his promised job. It seemed that we had been brought to a hostel on the other side of Melbourne, when there was another one that would have been much closer for him to his proposed place of work. Disoriented, he began to enquire of the hostel's staff how he would be able to reach his work each day. Perhaps it would be by public transport? Or maybe we would need to buy a car? All the options and their ramifications occupied his heart and mind.

And as he looked around, memories were stirred of a place long ago in Europe, of a time when he was also behind this type of fence. But there had been no freedom there, not like this new land. His dark eyes showed there was a black cloud descending, and his way of shutting out the world kicked in. A dark horse. Still waters running deep, unapproachable. Situations which ran out of his control always unnerved him.

THINK ABOUT THIS:

And in that he was so typical of any human being. We all want so much to think we are in control of our lives. The truth is that much of the time we struggle with the uncertainties of this life as much as the next person, but feel and believe the lie that we are the only one going through it.

We all want so much to think we are in control of our lives.

What is it about our Heavenly Father that is such a comfort? I think the fact that his thoughts and His mind are so accessible, that whenever we are unsure of what He is doing, thinking, or planning, we can actually turn to the pages of His Word. And it's there that we can hear Him speak to us inwardly.

We never need be concerned that God does not know the next step or that perhaps is making this all up as He goes! It's as though the Lord never wants to shut us out of His plans and purposes for us but continually assures us that His thoughts and actions are for us and not against us. He thinks of us all the time. Perhaps we don't know the future, perhaps we won't understand His ways and plans for us, but the fact that he is our refuge is enough.

We can easily succumb to our circumstances with the resultant fear and trepidation that it brings. But what is it that separates those of us with faith from those who don't trust and have any faith in God? Right here is where the answer 'kicks in': we can show, in times of uncertainty and stress, that we are able to draw on our strong Father for assurance and love. Safety, assurance, strength. Perhaps what every girl needs to know about her Father.

OVER TO YOU:

We will know His heart and His love when we believe His promises to us as we read the Bible. It's the Truth.

As we speak aloud positive words and believe only good for our future, the negative words of fear, which only pull us down, dissipate and fade. Speaking words of faith, hope and life give vision and substance to a great future. It's like turning on a light in a room; the darkness has to go. Let's allow the words of our Heavenly Father to dominate our minds when we're afraid or uncertain. They are the Truth.

Jeremiah 29:11

"For I know the plans I have for you," says the Lord. "They are plans for good and not for disaster, to give you a future and a hope".

Psalm 139:17, 19

How precious are your thoughts about me, O God! They are innumerable! I can't even count them; they outnumber the grains of sand!

Psalm 46:1

God is our refuge and strength, always ready to help in times of trouble.

Proverbs 18:10

The name of the Lord is a strong tower; the righteous run to it and are safe.

Father in Heaven,

There are so many times when my world crowds in around me, when it seems unfamiliar and I can only see the black clouds or the surrounding circumstances in all their negativity! Help me at these times to lift out of all this, to speak, act and know the Truth, which is that you have it all in your mighty hand, and I need to fear nothing. Amen.

Ten Pound Pom

New School, New Schoolbag!

The hooter sounded long and loud, a piercing interruption to the drone of my teacher's monologue. Every child in the room rushed to pick up a schoolbag, grabbing their picnic lunch that they'd brought from home. Some of the kids, armed with drink bottles which had been lovingly filled that morning by doting mums, headed out at breakneck speed into the playground, dashing to a well-loved corner or area where the rendezvous with friends would soon make the morning's dreary learning pace a distant memory.

The girls perched on old weatherworn wooden benches together, chattering like birds on a wire in the sun. Examining the contents of each other's lunches, they screwed up tiny noses or alternatively squealed with delight at a favourite menu presented before them. They exchanged the latest playground gossip and launched full flight into sisterly discussions on the happenings of the morning. Arm in arm they got up to wander, oblivious to the outside world, caught in the ca-maraderie of alikeness and aligning their female attitude to the world.

The boys gathered in groups around the grassed area (the 'oval' as they called it, though to me it appeared a very large rectangle, covered with a coarse and strange grass and some bright winter flowers). They spurred one another on to feats of strength and courage that any ten year old would consider a challenge. Sandwiches clasped in hand for a few seconds be-fore devouring them between kicks of the football, they knew that their very reputation would rest on the prowess and courage demonstrated in the playground that day. Success was rated by the number of grass stains on the shirt, the severity of a skinned knee and ripped shorts became trophies in the melee of these budding young sportsmen.

Arm in arm they got up to wander, oblivious to the outside world, caught in the camaraderie of alikeness and aligning their female attitude to the world.

Alone in the yard, I watched longingly as my schoolmates in this new and exciting place taught me silently the culture, communicat-ing without words the language of my new country. My mind flew to 'home' in England, and my Junior School playground. I had been often fondly engrossed in an 'acting game' of English history and heritage there. Usually I would be in the Oscar winning role of one of the ma-ligned wives of King Henry 8th, or some such historically important figure that I'd read about. Of course, I would also be the play's direc-tor! Often the plot involved the imprisoned Mary Queen of Scots, or the twin princes locked in the Tower of London. But these Australian kids knew nothing of my history-laden past and the stories of the centuries that are the inheritance of the English. Little did they understand the depth of isolation that the migrant could feel, the 'culture shock' that would come whilst that glittering promise of our bright future unfolded.

As I looked around the playground, there were small groups of immigrant children dotted around the outside of the 'main game'. They congregated together, particularly if mum had packed a lunch of 'international' foods. It was common for the Italian kids and the Greek kids (of which there were many) to congregate, eat and play together. Silently I stored impressions and learned how to relate to this foreign Australian people. The nuances of speech, the humour of a nation forged out of mateship and the excitement of building community from scratch in this ancient, yet new and fascinating country was all reflected in its children. And I began to hide my heritage, and became embarrassed at my different appearance, and the way that I spoke. I tried hard to forget the history of my home on the other side of the world. Both my brother and I tried to lose ourselves in the acceptance of our new peers. We watched and listened to one another as each one quickly took on board the character of the new speech and the ways and mannerisms of this people. It became a competition to lose the English accent fast!

Earlier that morning, eyes of all shapes, sizes and colours had been on me as I gingerly trotted behind Mrs Hampton down the corridor to my new classroom. Trying to keep up with her pace, I had listened intently between steps. The running commentary about the location of the 'shelter shed', the girls toilets and those important details to which she gave such preference, finally wound down as we arrived at the door to our classroom. A quiet buzz of children concentrating on their books had ceased as, one by one, they'd looked up laconically, with enquiring eyes. To them I was just another migrant child who was being brought in by the teacher, being routinely settled into the class. I'd felt the heat of their gaze as my face warmed slowly. Nervously I'd fiddled with the strap of my school satchel, as though plucking at it would relieve the intensity of this new experience, this affront at being the centre of attention. Quickly I'd taken in the scene. I'd never in my life seen a real live school desk and attached chair like this. Well, only in the Western movies that dad watched. Somewhat pew-like, I thought, as I'd tried to inconspicuously slide in and look cool and totally calm. Like I belonged.

Of course, I had been so very excited about the prospect of this day. My first day of Australian school! I had arrived with Mum by tram (such a foreign mode of transport—why ever didn't they have doors that close? Wouldn't it be dreadful in the dead of winter!) On boarding the tram that morning I had been reminded of the movies from long ago that I loved to watch. It was not unusual for me to retreat into my world of glamorous film stars and tingling story lines as I would imagine my lead role opposite some swashbuckling hero who would save me from a fate worse than death! And now as I rode the Melbourne tram my mind ran with images of childhood fantasy spurred on by the clanging of the driver on his bell, imitating the sound of the San Francisco trolley cars. My name was Jeanette, and I would, at any moment, burst into warbling song to the other passengers as I rocked in time with the motion of this trolley car clinging to the San Francisco hillside above a sparkling blue bay. But no, today this tram chugged through the Melbourne early morning traffic and transported us through the dull, overcast weather with only the promise of a brighter future. Better keep the song inside just now!

The class was used to receiving new kids. Close in proximity to the local Migrant Hostel at Maribyrnong in Melbourne, Victoria, it was an area used to extending its Australian hospitality to those new to its great shores. The local children had become accustomed to new additions from the local hostel arriving at intervals during the term. Hardly a head turned, really. And yet this was my entrance. So different to how I had imagined it before today. The kids here could wear anything to school. No more would I have to contend with the old brown pleated uniform of my former English school days. I had spent what seemed like an hour trying to pick out a suitable outfit for a ten year old to make their great Aussie school debut—oh, how I wanted to fit in! My blue velvet dress and long socks was a little out of place, somehow. And these kids were so tanned.

My brown leather English school satchel looked strange as it sat neatly next to these other colourful schoolbags, flung nonchalantly across the floor next to desks as though they had taken on the relaxed and humour-filled culture of their owners. The two national airlines at that time were marketed on bags. Brash advertising was splashed across their plastic exterior, pictures of aircraft inspiring the children who owned them to think of travel and other exciting things. There were so many different nationalities represented at the hostel. Europe's colourful profusion of languages, customs and dress were demonstrated every day in a procession of families as they stood at the tram stop to farewell children for the local primary school. But one thing we had in common. We had come to celebrate our freedom to live in a new and promise-filled country, which would benefit us as children and would prosper our own children and the generations to come. That was our hope.

The impact of this microcosm of life in the playground would set me in good stead as I started the journey towards becoming an Australian myself. From the mix of accents which floated in the air at lunchtime to the hesitant childish voices forming new and exciting words, we were constantly in an environment of learning, but always with a guarded tongue for fear of sounding odd. Never wanting to be outdone, I would try so hard to overcome what was 'different' and to fall into line with these healthy, confident Aussie kids who took things in their long stride and knew the ways of the world. Oh, to be like them, and not be stamped with the 'migrant' tag—it wouldn't take me long!

THINK ABOUT THIS:

What is it about us that wants to 'fit in'? Why do we feel the need to be 'in line' with those around us when God has created every one of us as a masterpiece, individual and creatively fashioned according to His likeness, and with His greatness tucked inside each one's DNA! How ungrateful it must seem that we want so desperately to hide our differences instead of celebrating them, to quell our creativity instead of encouraging it.

The Heavenly Father's heart is to see each of His daughters and sons reach their potential. I know that His heart is not to see us molded and shaped into the likeness of the culture that surrounds us. But often we fall into the trap of becoming the lonely, isolated 'new kid in the playground', aware of our differences of culture and language, highlighted by our lack of confidence and our inability to relate to those around us.

But God sees. And God knows. His heart is for us, with us, and able to not only transform us, but to relate to us when others cannot. Indeed, we are a complex creation!

OVER TO YOU:

You and I carry mind-blowing 'potential' that has been put inside of us by our Creator! What are we doing with it? We honour God when we are living each day according to what He has put within us. None of us the same, all of us with a 'special touch' from the Eternal One who cares so much for us!

You and I carry mind-blowing 'potential' that has been put inside of us by our Creator!

Could you let your own personal 'potential' spur you on to live your life differently to those around you? Living harmoniously, but writing your own 'song'? The One who loves you in Heaven is cheering you on! He's loving every one of those 'differences'.

What potential qualities do you think God has put within you?

Celebrate!

Psalm 139

Thank you for making me so wonderfully complex!

Your workmanship is marvelous—and how well I know it. You watched

me as I was being formed in utter seclusion,

As I was woven together in the dark of the womb,

You saw me before I was born.

Every day of my life was recorded in your book.

Every moment was laid out before a single day had passed.

Father in Heaven,

Help me to celebrate the fact that you've made me an individual, but you've made me according to your plan! Help me to learn to adapt to newness in my life, to love the growth and change that you bring, and to also celebrate others in their diversity. Amen.

A New Job

Shattered Dreams, Sorry Hearts

He was gazing out of the train's dusty window, and the city of Melbourne flew by at speed. Nervously he fingered the letter that had been written back in England by his supervisor recommending him for this new position. It was assured; he was to be employed at the plant and that was to be his launching pad into a new and exciting life of promise.

Bayswater, that was it, on the outskirts of the city of Melbourne. That was where he was headed. He went over in his mind again the much rehearsed speech that he would deliver to the new boss. He'd come half way around the world to do this. Had to be confident, had to be word perfect. Had to smile, look relaxed.

Drawing on his military background to present himself as well groomed, immaculately dressed and ready to work, he had begun his morning very early. Up at the crack of dawn, that was his way. He could almost still hear a lone soldier playing Reveille on a bugle outside his barracks. The discipline of such an ordered life had never left him. In the military it had never been good enough to present yourself as just 'OK'. You'd had to treat your appearance with exacting precision. You'd had to deal with every aspect of your military career in this way. Tweed sports jacket, matching well-pressed trousers and of course, mirror polished shoes. Even now Harry still presented as the soldier, *sir!* But He knew it would be a long journey today.

He would need to get a house for his young family out this way, start looking in the suburbs to provide for them all. A new life for his wife and two kids. A new start, with no past, no history, on the level of everyone else in this new society, this new country. He'd heard that this great land of Australia was the place to start again. And he was certainly going to give it all he had.

Railway stations, many with strange aboriginal-sounding names, whipped past as the train rhythmically loped out into a less populated area, filled with green fields and fresh air. A mountain range loomed closer in the distance. Ah! Here was the stop. The anticipation rose as he excitedly collected his coat next to him on the seat, and got up to meet the quickly approaching platform. He craned his neck to see the area around here, making sure that it was exactly where he meant to arrive. Smoothing his overcoat, precisely folded over one arm with the satin lining outermost, he thought about the future.

When he was nervous he would have a habit of squeezing his back teeth together in an action that formed a dimple in the side of his face. I watched this often, and knew that it meant he was not comfortable with the world then. Right now the dimple was working overtime! He braced one leg against the train's door, his mind racing to the interview ahead, as his fingers drummed the door's handle, showing his anxious heart. But though the adrenaline rose and he was excited about the chance ahead, he could not have anticipated what would happen next.

Just one hour later, he was the lonely figure standing at the end of that same platform. The colour in his face matched his grey trench coat, his shoulders drooped. His eyes held no promise for the future. Gone was the shine on tomorrow, closing in now was the dark cloud that was so very familiar. The crestfallen figure paced cold yards between the ticket box and the end of the concrete. He wondered how he was going to break this news to his wife. Full of regret and anger, his frustration seethed as he sucked his cheeks in hard, pulling the smoke and the life out of his cigarette. Quickly he fumbled for the packet in his coat pocket, lighting another one end to end, attempting to quell the rising anger and distress that mounted the attack and rose inside of him.

Now the train approached. He threw the cigarette aggressively down onto the cement, stepping onto it and grinding it harshly into the pavement. He would erase this day from his memory. But instead it burned furiously in his mind, like an uncontrolled bushfire that consumes and destroys everything in its path. Back to the other side now, back to the migrant hostel, back to the confines behind the barbed wire fence.

A soldier might have been able to crush his enemy and fight for all he was worth against the injustice of defeat, but now it was a different life. One where you couldn't fight back, one where you had to take this garbage and live to face another day, no matter who was trying to pull you down, no matter what was trying to steal your dignity and your future.

This job that he had come 12,000 miles to start, this job that his boss back home had promised: all of it was a lie! The interview had been a sham, an embarrassment, and when at the end of it the boss of the factory had offered him a job sweeping the floors, Harry had turned on his heel to walk out of there, and retain as much of his self respect as he could. They were all the same! Dad's reaction was just exactly why he had never risen to any dizzy heights in the British Army; he had always remained a private soldier. You couldn't trust any of the bosses. They'd all been out to use the rest of the workers. And as he muttered quietly to himself, his mood spiraled swiftly downward, sliding into darkness.

It had always been likely that he had been marching in time to a different drum. His memory reminded him of the countless times that he had put in long, hard hours working in the coalmines as a kid. With little or no pay he'd still had to obey the bosses who had mistreated him. Later on he had been subject to Nazi abuse in the Polish mines at the hands of an enemy who had kept his very freedom from him. As he turned the thoughts over and over in his heart, he became convinced that the demons would torment him even here in this new country. And as he left the station at Bayswater, he left behind a part of himself. He left behind his pride in his ability to provide for his wife and kids. He left behind faith in this new land, at least for now. He fought to regain hope.

What followed were several months of going for interviews, taking jobs that were never to give him the satisfaction he was looking forward to, never to be the fulfillment of the dream that had been meant to happen. It became familiar to hear him say, *"Well, I just put me coat on!"* Which meant, when he got angry at the boss, was done with the job, whatever it was, he would finish and walk out. Such was his lot, and maybe it would never change.

THINK ABOUT THIS:

It's always a choice whether or not to hold on to anger and frustration. Unforgiveness and a regret that eats into you as the years go by are often the result of injustice. And some of us handle that better than others. Perhaps some are better than others at sorting through life's expectations and the difference between them and reality.

In the heart of a father is the deep desire to care for his children. How heavily this responsibility weighed upon my own father! We can adopt rejection and learn to live with it as though it were meant to be a part of us. Life deals a blow and the anger and resentment rise. Slowly experiences can wear us down. My father became inwardly convinced that his portion in life was a rejection that would continue. It became a belief that needed constant feeding to exist, so he seemed to look for confirmation of that lie at every turn.

No matter what our experience in life is, or we can confidently run to the Lord. We can find safety there. We can choose what to expect. It may be to feel rejected or abandoned, or to allow our Father to embrace us. As I call, so He answers—the Father in the Heavens, whose heart is perfect, whose protection is constant, whose love is all encompassing.

OVER TO YOU:

Whatever your experience as a daughter, you can live in the Heavenly Father's love and care forever, without being afraid that it will be stolen from you.

> **Whatever your experience as a daughter, you can live in the Heavenly Father's love and care forever, without being afraid that it will be stolen from you.**

Your heart is safe, your life is precious to Him, your worth is guarded.

There is a choice: to believe and experience the life that God has for me, all the favour and blessing that is in His heart for me.

We need not look for life's experiences to *confirm* what we think we 'know' about our future. If we look to the Word of God to confirm who we really are, and what He has for us, we are then looking to the Truth.

Psalm 61: 1-4

> Hear my cry, O God; listen to my prayer. From the ends of the earth I call to you, I call as my heart grows faint; lead me to the rock that is higher than I. For you have been my refuge, a strong tower against the foe. I long to dwell in your tent forever and take refuge in the shelter of your wings. Selah

Father in Heaven,

Help me to hear what you are saying to me...every day! Your love and value need to be so totally in my head and my heart that I can persevere through any trial, victoriously battle any enemy, and continue to know that I have you and your unending love in my life always. Amen.

The Team

Marching Through Disappointment

She led the squad of identically clad young ladies, all with eyes focused in the same direction, marching to the beat in measured steps, their arms swinging to the same height, their heads turning first right then left in staccato movement together. The captain twirled and again tossed her baton high into the sky, and in one victorious movement snatched it back to earth, leading her company to a spectacular finish that was greeted by great applause from watching parents and friends on the sidelines.

Dressed in short red tunics with black ties around their waists, white ankle socks and tennis shoes, the company of girls stepped crisply in time to the music and executed with precision their practiced routine. A satisfied teacher looked on with glowing admiration, peering over her bifocals at the gathering of besotted parents standing by. As if to demonstrate her worth because of her young charges' performance, she demonstratively clapped her hands as the girls took a bow.

I hadn't been in Australia very long, but realized that this is what I wanted to be. A marching girl! The music inspired me to be a part of this somewhat unusual 'sport', and coaxed me to join with the girls who happily drilled for hours after school just to make the team. And finally, after weeks of ambitious 'try outs' and never quite making the grade, I had been given a place as a reserve for the State School marching girls team! My joy was unspeakable! It was all very well to have a brother who was good at school work, but when they also outshone you in sporting endeavours, well, that was too much! Here was a sport that I could qualify for just *because* I was a girl! Even though I was the shortest in height, my teacher had given me a chance, and I was going to prove my worth!

The day of the school's competition arrived, and everyone was ready to give it their best shot. I had never really been a part of any team sports, so the camaraderie and team spirit was a new experience, one that touched a deep part of me and encouraged my sense of belonging in a new country. We had all donned our scarlet uniforms and looked a striking company of girls as we practised formations on the tarmac before the carnival. The coach had placed me as the last on the line, due to my being the shortest, so I led the 'winding and unwinding' exercise, which was to be my proudest moment! We had spoken about it all as a family at breakfast that morning. I was overjoyed when dad had said he was going to try his very best to be there himself for my shining performance.

I couldn't wait till classes for the morning were finished. Racing through a lunch of sandwiches and fruit, quickly eaten at the shelter shed, I thought back to the 'old days' in England where most of the time the weather was too cold to venture out into the playground in the winter, and 'school dinners' were a vastly different proposition: overcooked, limp vegetables and desserts of custard and sponge cake. But the picnic lunches packed especially for me by the migrant hostel kitchen workers were so different and exciting!

We were about to perform, and dad had arrived to watch me. What a proud moment.

How I loved my new country, its interesting customs and strange and intriguing ways. I just wanted to be a part of it all, be involved in everything Australian! And being a marching girl just *had* to be one of the rites of passage that I had passed through with flying colours! Nothing, simply nothing, seemed more important than performing with 'The Squad'!

We were around half way through the festival's program when a car that looked just like the one dad had been driving as a chauffer for a big company, motored lazily into the dead-end street, coming to a stop outside the school gate. I could see it from where I was, waiting in line. It was a big, black Pontiac; you couldn't miss my dad! But the sun was just in the wrong spot, so I couldn't quite see his face. I waved excitedly anyway. We were about to perform, and dad had arrived to watch me. What a proud moment.

Our routine was grand, the applause loud, and we finished our item with such a sense of achievement. The moment done, I raced towards the cluster of parents on the lawn, searching the faces eagerly for my own dad, to collect his encouragement and compliments like a congratulatory bouquet of flowers. But he was nowhere to be seen. The big black car still languished outside the gate in the same position—with nobody inside. But Dad was not there. Just at that moment I watched as a couple of happy parents made their way over to the waiting vehicle, and my heart sank as I realized that my Dad had not even arrived to watch me today. That car belonged to somebody else. My heart sank.

I know that the oversight was unintentional. I also know that the disappointment was hard to come to terms with. We each need to move on from those times, but it's a hard lesson in the heart of many a child to realize that life disappoints, and so do fathers.

THINK ABOUT THIS:

How do you overcome disappointment when an earthly father lets you down? Well, many of us learn that lesson early, and this story is just one of many that could illustrate the point. You might say, "But every one lets their kids down. Just get over it!" And of course, you would be right. But when we 'just get over it' we tend to bury the hurt along with the incident.

And many people have incidents of 'let down' that are so much greater than this one, but the hurt always goes down deep, with its descent gathering to itself every other time that we have been let down. The package lands with a resounding thump at the 'bottom' of our hearts, that heavy combination of weary hurt affirming our lack of esteem on the inside. And there it sits, sinker-like, as in the depths of an ocean of broken dreams, waiting for the Discoverer to dig it out of the deep hiding place, exposing it to the Light that heals.

The trouble is that hurt is a bit like nuclear waste: it takes a very, very long time to break down, if ever, without a miracle. But there is something that can help us to get rid of hurt. And that agent, in the case of hurt, is my Heavenly Dad. And something that He shows us is possible. It's called for-giveness.Overcoming the disappointment that earthly relationships will inevitably bring is actually not possible unless we have somewhere to store the hurt. Knowing that we can bury our hurt in the arms of the Heavenly Dad makes up for the devastation of knowing that humanity carries with it the certainty of failure. But God never fails.

We will often fail others, and others will often fail us. What we do with the hurt that follows involves making a life-altering choice.

And if we trust in Him and make sure our lives are constantly open to Him, He will show us how to throw off the hurt and disappointment, how to be healed of this and its eventual devastating effects of a lack of belief in ourselves.

OVER TO YOU:

God can help with your hurt. Open up your heart to Him today in prayer, and ask His help in learning both forgiveness and trust. It's a simple matter of asking.

We will often fail others, and others will often fail us. What we do with the hurt that follows involves making a life-altering choice.

Make a brave choice to not take your hurt and 'nurse' it, but to allow the Heavenly Father to reach in and take the hurt away, replacing it with His peace.

2 Corinthians 4:8

When I am pressed on every side by troubles, I am not crushed and broken. When I am perplexed because I don't know why things happen as they do, I don't give up and quit.

Psalm 22:5

In you they trusted and were not disappointed

Ephesians 4:32

Be kind and compassionate to one another, forgiving each other, just as in Christ God forgave you.

Heavenly Father,

Many times people have hurt me—although not always knowingly and on purpose. But the more it happens, the more I can build up the walls that kill communication in relationship. Help me to be open, to understand that no matter how many times I am disappointed by others I can always turn to the ONE who understands. I give You all my hurt. Help me to let it go. Replace it with your peace. Amen

Surefooted

Balancing A Life

"He's as sure footed as a mountain goat!" My friend Alison declared her admiration of this middle aged man who had come to her aid and carried her across to the house. He picked his way across the wet clay yard that was littered with building materials as construction sites often are. Carrying Alison to the house and gently setting her down on our new verandah with a flourish, he clapped his hands in a motion that indicated he had finished the task with satisfaction. He looked around with a wry grin, dark eyes dancing, and called "Next?"

For their whole lives the dream of owning their own home had eluded Mum and Dad, but here, finally, was a chance to do that. In the north of the city of Adelaide, basically in the middle of a country area, surrounded by market gardens and farming communities, most of whom had emigrated from southern Europe, they chose to buy their first home. What an achievement that was! Migrating from another country, bringing up two kids, changing lifestyles, culture and outlook, they had literally turned all our lives upside down.

It wasn't really very long after that, I will always remember, that things started to spiral downward for my dad. Looking pale and worn one afternoon, as he had been trying to dig into the harsh South Australian clay soil to make a new garden bed for Mum, he'd leant on his spade with a relaxed arm, taking a break from his labour. Trying his best to appear nonchalant, I could see the sweat beading rapidly on his forehead and then running down the side of his face, creating tiny paths as it collected the dust and dirt of the day's digging. Now reaching quickly into a pocket to retrieve his handkerchief, he'd wiped his brow with a dabbing motion over his not uncommon frown. I recall clearly how I'd watched him and wondered what on earth made him continue, when he had clearly had enough much earlier in the day. I shook my head slowly as I asked myself the big question. Surely he must have been breathless and overcome with the pain in his chest that was so obviously there? His heart was no doubt by now giving signals that this was more than he should be doing.

A few short years before, dad had announced that all of us were to move from Melbourne to the island of Tasmania, where he had secured his latest job offer. Along with a veritable army of men he would be instrumental in starting up the new aluminium plant at Bell Bay. Hard work never frightened him, nor did commitment, but this was to be a big project. It wasn't long before his heart started to weaken, and the angina and heart pains began. I remember one day coming home from my first days of High School and walking into the lounge, where he'd been brought home from yet another spell in the local hospital, now becoming a regular occurrence.

He'd looked small, fragile, almost elf-like. Reclining in the lounge armchair, my father sighed deeply and closed his eyes for a moment, taking in all that he had just returned to. His home, his family. After a close call, a major heart attack and two months in hospital, the strain was obvious in his eyes. He had lost a lot of weight. The glitter and excitement was gone from those dark brown eyes, and his hair had become much more grey, and plainly very much thinner where there had not so long ago been a thick, dark, curly mass.

The weeks that had gone before had been dream-like, impacting. After Dad's collapse and admission to hospital, we would visit him every night. Mum had been nervous about driving there, so we'd walked the steep hill to the Launceston hospital each evening after she'd come home from work. And quite often on the way home, my brother had to push us up the hill again to get us back to the house!

As dad had started to get better and become a little chirpier at the hospital, the ward nurses had got to know him. It seemed he'd been the life of the party, the guy who arranged all the patients' wheelchair races! And quite often the staff would roll their eyes and smile as they described the antics of this recovering ex-soldier, as they related the day's happenings to us during our visits. He really knew how to enjoy himself.

But life had changed now, outside the hospital. He was no longer able to provide for his family, to work towards their future. This reality had now begun to set in, and all this so soon after arriving in this new country. He felt the

He felt the frustration of this reality often, and it showed in his mood and in his eyes.

frustration of this reality often, and it showed in his mood and in his eyes. The air would so carry this lack of confidence in himself now that you could almost feel it.

And as I watched him this day in the garden, he slowly, almost elegantly, fell backwards. His spade dropped with a thud onto the hard soil. It was like a slow motion movie. I could do nothing but yell for Mum, who sprang into action. The teapot dropped from her hand, and she ran out to the garden. *"Harry, Harry, are you all right?"*

And as the ambulance drove away with Dad in the back, yet again, I sighed, took a deep breath and picked up his spade. This type of thing was becoming a regular event. The hospital run with Dad was always traumatic, always brought with it the fear of uncertainty to our daily lives. But as disruptive and frightening as it was, it was also very familiar now.

As I picked up his gardening tools, I wondered why. Why did he always need to be doing these things that he could no longer do? Why not just accept the fact that he could no longer do them all? How could he continue to do this to us? Dad was the kind of man who continually tried, continually pushed the barriers that tried to close in on him—his health, his aging, his life. He was just not a 'quitter'.

But the effect of his illness was not just on him alone. A family lives with chronic illness all together and feels its effects corporately. It is not just the patient who suffers.

Dad seemed to carry an invisible mantle that drove him towards squeezing the very marrow out of life, living the moments for so much more than they were worth, valiantly taking whatever was dealt with the characteristic bravery that perhaps carried him during his war experience. There was no accusing this man of "taking up space on the planet…" He wanted to live every moment to the maximum. And so this latest chapter of his life, slowing him down so much, was hard to take. It was as though his soul was dying within.

THINK ABOUT THIS:

Sometimes I can lose my way, and tend to want to give up. When I feel lost like that, I have learned that I can listen for that soft prompting on the inside. It's not a voice. It's a stirring. It's a confidence that Someone is looking out for me. And it's then that I remember this man, this rugged character with the swarthy olive skin and dark, dark eyes. This man who, though he loved me, sometimes did not know how to express that. This man who acted and reacted according to his experience, his hurt, his past, but appeared never to have known how to hear and take note of the stirring of the One who cares.

Though I've found it frustrating and at times questioned why anyone would continue to 'push through' in life when it clearly hurt so much and caused pain, I have to say that it is an admirable trait and one that appeared so often in my father. That dogged determination to keep going. Occasionally I have wished that he'd been a man of balance, instead of extremes.

Balance is precious. Without it, Jesus would have worn Himself out on the Earth. He took time out to surrender his heart to his Father and to solitude. And he often encouraged his disciples to do the same. Many a daughter will lose her trust because of the man who is her father. Perhaps he makes her annoyed, frustrated or just plain mad! But we can't use our opinion of our father, our genetics, or our environment for all the negatives in our lives! We can't allow a lack of trust because we were let down in the past. It can't be a basis for our allowing ourselves to play the 'blame game' in our future.

It's all a matter of balance. A balance in our emotions allows us to 'grow up' into what God has ready for us. And He does indeed have a 'plan' for all of us daughters!

"Own your stuff" we hear often. That's a thought-provoking exercise! As we transition from 'little girl' to 'grown up person' and attend to the areas of growth that Father God puts His finger on and says, "how about we deal with this?..". That's when we learn balance.

There is a freedom in trusting my Heavenly Father.

There is a freedom in trusting my Heavenly Father. There's a balance that brings home the sweet journey into maturity that He can lead us in, if we will just trust Him!

It's not a misplaced trust. Every day I need some 'time out' with just Him and me. That has been the saving grace of my life. Just to surround myself with his love and to worship Him on my own has been the thing that has held me safe and centred, balanced—day after day. Some call it 'self care'. I call it falling back into my Heavenly Dad's arms and just being…

OVER TO YOU:

Pushing the boundaries and therefore pushing yourself too far often results in an effect that 'ripples' out to others who are significant in your life.

Remember that we will impact others negatively if we don't positively look after ourselves. Make your health a priority, particularly your emotional health.

Losing our 'balance' in life will almost certainly cause us to fall. You know you are 'out of balance' when your emotions are ruling your life. You know they are ruling your life when that 'peace' is missing. If that is happening to you today, then take some 'time out' to read the scriptures below, and have a little chat with your Heavenly Dad, who, though you cannot see him, hears you and can change things for you.

Psalm 84

My soul longs, yes, even faints

For the courts of the Lord:

My heart and my flesh cry out for the living God.

Matthew 11:28

Are you tired? Worn out? Burned out on religion? Come to me. Get away with me and you'll recover your life. I'll show you how to take a real rest. Walk with me and work with me—watch how I do it. Learn the unforced rhythms of grace. I won't lay anything heavy or ill-fitting on you. Keep company with me and you'll learn to live freely and lightly".

Father in Heaven,

I read in the Bible that I can trust you. But my human experience quite often tells me the opposite. So now I am asking for help, Lord. Help me to learn this new trust and help me to learn the dignity of being sure-footed in my faith in You. My Rock. My Redeemer. My Rest. Teach me to trust You. Teach me the balance of the 'unforced rhythm' of trusting you in my life. Amen

20 Uncanny Rhythm

The Melody of Encouragement

It was Dad's habit to scour the morning newspaper for anything unusual, often becoming so engrossed that he almost left the room for a bit, departing from present company. He would sit, peering though the bottom of his spectacles with angled chin, frowning and trying to see more clearly through his cumbersome bifocals.

This particular day he'd noticed a small advertisement. It had immediately caught his imagination. Often he would sit, concentrating, busily nibbling on his fingernails as he became a part of the world within the print. Novels would transport him to another dimension. Newspapers would take his attention totally. And his ever-present cigarette would patiently smolder in the ashtray as he momentarily lost interest in it:

"Scholarships from the Adelaide College of Music, offering ten free lessons on the guitar for talented students…audition required".

He was thinking of his daughter's fifteenth birthday coming up in June. He picked up his lit cigarette, gently tapped it on the green glass ashtray sitting at his elbow, and skilfully, thoughtfully, pulled it up to his mouth in a single, seemingly unconscious movement. Exhaling curls of blue smoke, he balanced it lovingly beside him on the ashtray's side and carefully tore out the advert from the paper. He placed it aside, smoothing it on the kitchen table as he pondered on what it would mean. Probably have to buy her a guitar. Probably have to take her into the college soon, in order to grab one of these special deals. She could win a scholarship. Musical child.

Slowly a memory came back to him. It was from the old country, some eight years ago now, when mum and he had travelled to The Cotswolds to a picturesque village called Winchcombe. Again, Dad had been browsing the local paper and had noticed a tiny ad in one of the back pages that appealed to him and set him off on one of his 'quests' towards getting a real bargain for his daughter.

Climbing high in the hills in dad's beat up old Austin, the journey had finally ended in a tiny street. Cozily nestled into a corner of the village, away from the hustle of the shopping area and perched gently at the edge of town just before the fields and countryside started again, there was a tiny cottage. It was perched like an afterthought on a small hill at the end of a narrow cobbled street. This appeared to be where the newspaper advertisement had led us. Excited to be a part of the adventure and running hastily from the car as soon as we had stopped, I approached its wooden door, complete with peeling paint and a brass doorknocker shaped like a horseshoe. Eagerly I'd rapped on it as hard as I could.

From inside the house came a stirring and a patter of slippered feet before a little old man with kind, gentle manner had opened the door a crack. On hearing the explanation of our mission, he'd smiled slowly and opened the door, inviting us in and leading us up a narrow staircase to a tiny attic room at the top of the little house. Now as we crowded into the room, dad bowing low so as not to crack his head on the close, angled ceiling, I'd noticed that there was a beautiful little instrument laid out carefully on the top of a neatly made bed. Oh, so *that* was what a ukulele-banjo looked like!

The old man had been delighted that his treasured instrument was finally going to a good home, and painstakingly showed me how to tune it. When

The best way he knew how to encourage was to give.

he had thoroughly explained its operation and care, it was gently laid into its old and somewhat frayed blue leather case. He smiled again at the little girl who would take it home. A little later, when negotiations were done, he had somewhat wistfully and with a soft West-country brogue bid farewell at the front door to the little family from Cheltenham. Clambering back into the car, I remember turning and waving at the small back window, clutching my new treasure, until the cottage was finally out of sight.

Adelaide, South Australia, was experiencing one of its famous desert heat waves, and as such was so very far removed from England. Today's mission was to possess a guitar, so different from the experience of eight years previously, but somehow still the same. Dad was still wanting to encourage my love of music, doing all that he was able to do to help me enjoy it. The best way he knew how to encourage was to give.

The audition was fairly straightforward, a testing of rhythm, count and pitch. Easy for me, who loved music and had been appreciating it since the days when Dad would tap his feet and suck his pipe to the Swing record coming out of the radio at home. Nervously I sat on my own outside the small office as Dad listened intently to the teacher giving him the results of my test. *"An uncanny sense of rhythm she has!"* The drummer in my dad rose up from the inside, and pride spread generously across his face as he realized his hand in that talent. Genetics!

That guitar was a source of pleasure and learning for many years to come. As I sat excitedly through my 'free' ten lessons and learned how to form chords, strum rhythmically and sing along with the old favourites that we were taught in class, I began to believe a bit more in myself. Every week I eagerly looked forward to the trip into Adelaide to learn more about my new instrument, feeling as though I had finally found *the* talent of my life! I could feel my self-esteem rising with every lesson, every new song, every test that I took along with my fellow students. Chatting with my instructor after lessons, it seemed that I had found a new friend. His encouragement I valued so much. So, of course, my teacher got to hear about my life.

At that time my Dad had been hospitalized again and was experiencing heart attacks more frequently. Due to the stress of Dad's illness Mum was now suffering from a full-blown disease which debilitated her greatly. As her joints swelled and her movements became inhibited, she struggled to deal with rheumatoid arthritis. Every other month, it seemed, she also was being hospitalized or tested medically with new treatments and drugs.

In the midst of this life shone the oasis of my much-valued weekly guitar lessons. My instructor at the college was a friendly and jovial middle-aged man who had, it seemed, much compassion and insight. I felt as though I had been adopted in a sense. I wasn't quick to pick it up, but after a number of weeks I began to realize that he was generously extending the number of lessons that I had been entitled to, without saying a word. Ten lessons turned into eleven, to thirteen, now fifteen! The lessons continued on and on, until I had around me a completely new set of students. My teacher's kindly thoughtfulness, week by week, made an impression. His young student curiously pondered how lucky she had become.

Dad was, like any father, wanting to do the best for his child. In his own way he knew he wanted to leave his daughter a legacy, though there was much that he had already given without even knowing it. He had acted upon a generous impulse and given something to me that tangibly changed how I thought of myself, allowing me to skill-up in an area that was previously never thought of, and up until then a closed door to me. In turn, it was one I could benefit from by stepping into a fresh sense of value. I started to see that perhaps even I could have untapped talent that could be enjoyed and acted upon in order to enrich myself, and even others!

My dad has been gone for decades. But that guitar still sits in my lounge room today. It is often picked up and played by my son. Its language is love. It represents the heart of a Father for his daughter. My ukulele-banjo is a treasure that is now probably antique, and hangs on my wall, a silent reminder of a place of the past and a gift of encouragement.

THINK ABOUT THIS:

At times when the rage was quiet inside his mind, my father could appreciate that life was short, and his influence on this earth was important. He would do what appeared to be random acts of generosity and kindness, like this, that showed the heart of the Heavenly Father so clearly. The emotion would sparkle in his dark eyes, and his soul would tell a story without words through his actions.

Generosity lived on the inside, struggling so hard to get out. But the generous heart that was in there was so often masked by what the world had imprinted on his life. This mask was like a hallmark, a seal permanently stamped, seemingly immovable, except when a deed like this happened to break the deadlock in his mind.

The human heart craves love. But we understand love so dimly most of the time. It's the commitment to love that drives us to a generosity that echoes the giving heart of our Heavenly Father. So often the demonstration of the acts of kindness that are born out of the commitment of love can last a lifetime. They can influence generations!

It's the commitment to love that drives us to a generosity that echoes the giving heart of our Heavenly Father.

In life, we can look around at this world of beauty and see the Heavenly heart that is committed to us, is delighted in us.

OVER TO YOU:

Be generous, particularly to those you love. Maybe past experience appears so strong that you find yourself being inhibited, so you don't hear the prompting on the 'inside' that would give you the liberty to be generous. Encouragement is nothing more than 'putting courage into' another. It is the ultimate gift, and is generosity in itself, because you are lifting up another and allowing them to shine.

Who can you encourage today?

John 3:16

For God so LOVED the world, that He GAVE his only son....

Father in Heaven,

There are times when I become so tied up in who and what I am, that I forget the power that is in me to encourage others in my life. Help me to remember that a generous heart and spirit reflects the love of my Creator. Amen.

The Final Goodbye

Free At Last

A dull spring Thursday morning. September 3rd. The first thing that I remember was a shocked awakening as Mum called me, shaking my arm as I slowly came out of slumber. *"Quick, I can't wake your Father!"*

Though bleary eyed, I remember being shocked awake and following her to the lounge room where Dad had been sleeping at night now for some time in order to breathe warm air from the heater. Many years working in coalmines had resulted in a form of silicosis creeping into his lungs. It was an insidious disease that gradually and unlawfully took over the organs supporting his very life. This was coupled with a diseased heart and other ailments that had resulted from his war experience especially. His body had slowed to a lesser pace from the time we had arrived in Australia, and we were now used to seeing him fight off life-threatening situations.

But this morning we could see his still body lying in the bed, arms neatly folded across his chest. The expression on his lifeless face almost spoke out that he'd known death was on the approach for him. It was as though he knew it was going to happen. Completely peaceful and almost welcoming; such was his repose that morning.

No answer to our cries now. No response to our desperate calls and shaking of his body. Just sweet peace. No normal stretch and yawn as he awoke to face the world for another day. Nothing. An absence of movement. An absence of presence. An absence of life. As Mum quickly gathered herself, adrenalin took over. Quickening her pace, she ran out the door to a neighbour's house to phone a doctor. And I was left alone.

The silence threw a cold and dark blanket over everything that wanted to breathe and move. My heart was now the only thing I was aware of. Its beat was quick and loud. I was so acutely aware of its continuing to keep time inside me. It echoed its constant rhythm in my ears as it beat, almost, through the walls of my chest.

I've heard people say that at times of extreme stress such as this, time seems to pass in 'slow motion'. This day was just like that, and I don't struggle to remember any of those few moments. They are as indelibly printed in my memory as any moment of supreme importance that I have ever lived.

I heard myself confessing to the silent room that I was sorry, so very sorry, for having lied to him. Giving voice to past fears and insecurities, the words rushed up from inside and hit the air like an explosive river in flood. It swelled and came up and out of my mouth in confession. Like a torrent that could not be held back. A reckless wave that needed to be given expression, needed to be told. This was all about me and what I had done to cut his life short.

Allowing panic to reign, and insecurity to drown me, I sank to the depths of unbelief as I searched for some meaning to the events that were now spiraling out of control. I remember thinking that this was too early and it wasn't meant to happen now. And what mattered to me most was the fact that I had not said "goodbye". I was shattered to think that I would never hear his voice, touch his hand, link eye to eye with him, again. And it mattered that I had never had the chance to say it. That word "goodbye".

And now my life would be lived without him, without his influence, without his protection. As I clutched at a nearby curtain, my face became drenched with tears. Heaving sobs waved over me in a torrent of unleashed emotion. I sank down to hit the floor in despair.

The storm lasted until Mum finally returned from her mission to get help. She seemed so in control, so able in this situation. And I was so obviously devastated. In an error of judgment that would take decades to correct, my little girl's heart was wrenched from inside me and spilled out into an empty room where my Father lay dead. The error, or the lie that I believed, was to haunt me for so many years. It was to be the deepest reason and need in my search for love. It was the mistaken belief that I needed to make things right in my life by searching for the approval that I must have to be complete. Dad had left before I'd felt his approval. I had to prove somehow that this final abandonment was not justified, or fair. So relationships from this day on were a journey of frustration and anger, as I tried to remedy the hurt that was the abandonment of this day.

Decades later, at a conference in South America, I actually allowed my Heavenly Father to touch this deep and hurting wound in my heart. Emotional pain, without significant and remedial exposure and then healing, can easily be covered up so that the healing that is needed is not received. The day that I let my Father in Heaven pull these experiences out of my soul, I understood the difference between Him and my earthly dad. Forgiveness flowed, understanding brought peace, and the love of my Heavenly Father eclipsed all the judgment and despair that had crept into my teenage heart that dark day. That day, I was finally healed.

September 3rd 1944, was declared St Valery Day in France to celebrate its liberation by the Allies. It was the day that the armies marched in to free the people of a captive nation, many of the soldiers being from dad's 51st Highland Division.

September 3rd 1970. A significant day, when my daddy passed into Eternity; finally liberated from the sadness that always haunted him and caused a tormented heart and spirit, now finally at rest with his Creator.

THINK ABOUT THIS:

For those daughters who have suffered abuse at the hand of a father, who have been left with shattered dreams and hopes because of the under-valuing of themselves in the eyes of perhaps the most important person in their lives, a relationship with our Heavenly Father can release untapped potential, can help to cause untapped beauty of soul to flourish. Only He has the ability to wipe away the hurt, the negative images and the damage that may have been impressed upon her.

OVER TO YOU:

Many of us view God through the tinted windows of our own biased and sometimes battered souls. Be honest now: list the qualities that you may have attributed to God the Father but which you know do not apply to Him. (The picture that we see of this magnificent Heavenly Father is often contrary to His true appearance and nature.)

Many of us view God through the tinted windows of our own biased and sometimes battered souls.

We can use the magnifying glass of our own experience to see God in our own image. Better, though, if we understand that we are created in His image. Can you imagine yourself becoming more like Him?

We can and often do use the measuring stick of relationships on Earth to evaluate how, and even if, we can relate to God. They are not even comparable.

Psalm 23

> The Lord is my shepherd, I have everything I need.
> He lets me rest in green meadows;
> He leads me beside peaceful streams.
> Even when I walk through the dark valley of death,
> I will not be afraid,
> For you are close beside me.
> Your rod and your staff protect and comfort me.

Father in Heaven,

I cannot understand life and death. How can I, when much of it is spiritual and not discernible? Help me, Lord, to trust in your higher knowledge, power and protection. Let me understand this: that your GRACE, all your forgiveness and all your favour, is all I need to know. And that brings a freedom beyond words. Amen.

22 A Soldier's Farewell

The Arrival Home

That I was never able to say 'goodbye' to dad was all that mattered now. Life had taken a turn in its road, and we were rolling down the track of our future at breakneck speed. That was the feeling as I awoke to an overcast day in September, much like the day before—an eternity ago. Circumstances closing in made me feel like I was out of control. Today was to be the start of a life so different, a life without my father.

It had been about ten o'clock two evenings ago, that I'd returned from a drama class with a local repertory company. I'd noticed dad inside the house. Putting my key into the lock I'd absent-mindedly opened the front door. Turning towards the lounge room window, I'd been able to just make out through the voile curtains that he was still awake and sitting in his favourite chair in front of the TV. He'd probably been waiting up for me. I was still full of the buzz from the night's activity, my head still immersed in character from the part that I'd been reading for an audition in the amateur production that was on offer at a local theatre. So much for arriving home unnoticed.

Flinging a casual "Hi Dad" in his direction, I'd headed directly to the fridge in the kitchen and taken a half empty bottle of lemonade out, pouring it into a glass. Realizing that Dad had bought this small treat for himself, I'd stopped pouring and turned towards the other room, feeling obliged to ask his permission to take some.

"Fine" came his quiet word from the lounge room. A smile had spread from his eyes down to his mouth, as he'd turned his head towards me. Cigarette in hand, he'd been noticeably kind and peaceful that night.

"Thanks Dad".

And that, forever, had been our final exchange.

Thirty-six hours later, I was still unable to process the events that had happened. It was at once exhilarating and yet frightening.

And that, forever, had been our final exchange.

Feelings were up one moment and down the next. Emotional storms could not be timed or controlled, but were wild and sudden, like a beast that overtook, threatening better judgment at the most inappropriate of times. Tears flowed then ebbed away. Adrenalin rushed in and out like a restless tide on the sand.

Our local funeral director, a dark haired, stocky man with gentle demeanor, assisted Mum well and helped her navigate through this most difficult of events. He had a Greek surname and a strong Australian accent. Sometimes, the details of a momentous occasion can be remembered more clearly than in its overall effect. Small characteristics can become the most prominent memories. Arrangements were hurriedly made because the weekend approached, and it was inconvenient to prolong the farewell until the following week. Or that's what we were told.

The next day, an impressive black and shiny limousine drew up to our little suburban house around mid morning. As I was helped into the back seat, I remember thinking how like the Pontiac it was that dad used to drive in Melbourne. I slid across the shiny, polished leather. Tinted windows could hide tired, bereaved faces—a purpose-built transport for those who grieved. With a distant, professional smile, the driver gently closed the door as I got a last look at the rain-heavy sky.

Mum sat next to me in the back, looking lovely and poised, new hairdo complimenting her smart black suit. She'd paid attention to the detail of her appearance, saying to me that Dad would have wanted her to look smart and not 'sloppy' in front of our friends that special day. But behind the sunglasses she hid a painful realization that this was the beginning of a very different life. For all her husband had been, she'd cared for him deeply.

We drove into a small car park at the side of the chapel. Somberly dressed friends of the family waited for us. Greetings came in emotional bursts, pastel-toned and hushed. There were even some people from my work place gathered there to stand with me. How did they know? How could they care? Curious.

Walking into the small, pale-bricked building, we were warmly greeted by Father Ayles, our local Anglican priest. He clutched a Bible under one arm as he leaned down and extended a sympathetic hand to my mother. He had been visiting Dad for some weeks now, and had become very much a respected but familiar part of our world. His eyes settled on mine, and communicated a sense of sympathy. His smile was genuine and caring, so the unnecessary words lingered in the air, unsaid but understood. I felt my heart look to him for strength.

I remember to this day his words that Dad had 'made his peace with God'. It gave me an undeniable sense of comfort to hear it, during the brief eulogy. I have recalled those words for years. The comfort that they bring is twofold: being helpful to smooth creased and forgotten memories of a father who left too soon; and fuelling a hope to a meeting in eternity sometime in the future. Apart from the priest's words, I don't remember much from the eulogy. I do remember the beautiful sheaths and bouquets of flowers, and the playing of The Last Post by the bugler who stood to the side of where we sat. A soldier's farewell and a soldier's right, to have the tune played in his honour. I still find it difficult to listen to this piece, without thinking of my dad. On that day, as the tune came to an end, silence enveloped the small group of mourners. The music hung uncomfortably on the air.

Ushers directed the family up the aisle and out into the garden. But my eyes were fixed on the coffin as my emotion caught up. Unable to tear myself away from its side, I allowed another wave of painful sorrow to overtake me. It nailed me to the spot, and, unable to move, I began to comprehend a little more the empty regret of wanting to say goodbye, but knowing that I never would.

In recent years, Dad had been a member of the "39ers", a group of ex soldiers who had been in the Dunkirk battle of World War II. Each one had the right to a small canister of sand that had been brought from that little French beach. Each soldier, in turn as they passed away, had their canister buried with them. It was a significant ritual. A touching ceremony dedicated to honouring those who had fought far away from home on a foreign beach one day in June, 1940. Dad had been one of the last soldiers to leave that battlefield. Now he was one of the last soldiers from that battle to leave Earth.

Sadly, slowly, we began to file out first as the family in procession. But with Dad's coffin open, I just had to take a long and last look. I stood still, as did time. Being next to his lifeless body on this final occasion, I wish I could say that memories flooded into my mind of our time together. But, truthfully, my mind was empty. The air was empty. He looked unlike the dad I had known. Gone were the smile and the shine on his dark skin. Gone forever the gaze of dark brown eyes that danced as he would share a funny episode of "Hogan's Heroes" on our little black and white TV with me. I would never hear his infectious chuckle again. My heart would nevermore feel the pang of sorrow and regret at his depressive moods.

As we finally came out of the chapel, the sun shone down on my head, and I felt an angry pang of resentment that it wasn't raining. People gathered around us as we dried our eyes and set our hearts towards an uncertain future. I felt an empathetic hand at my elbow, heard a word of sympathy to my mother at my side.

When we reached home, I distanced myself from the people who had come to be with us, and found myself on dad's bed, his wardrobe open in front of me. I pressed his clothes into my face. Perhaps to continue to remember, maybe to regret what had gone on. Maybe it was to whisper what had never been said, perhaps to remind myself never to forget.

It was around six months later that we interned dad's ashes in the little churchyard attached to Saint John's Anglican Church. A beautiful sandstone structure that had weathered over a hundred years, it was a lovely place to put the memories to rest. This peaceful cemetery, this quiet little church outside Adelaide, was home to graves from up to a century before. Many soldiers had been buried here; many families had brought loved ones home to this final resting place.

Mum had been able to have dad's soldier's badge from the British Army, a bronze piece that glittered now in the sun, set into the concrete head stone at his cremation plot. The morning was a gathering of our closest family and was a final farewell to Harry, the soldier. Harry the husband. And of course, Harry the father.

But the passing months, then years, began to steal the raw feelings, and, though I wanted to let them go, I felt the same fascination with them as I had done the day of the funeral standing by his coffin. It was hard to release memories and feelings that connected you to someone. And the more I learned to live without him, the easier it was to forget him. But that meant forgetting the sound of his voice, his peculiar northern English accent, the touch of his hand.

I visited the small grave one day the following summer. As I walked pensively through the little cemetery, the memories that I had buried for a short time were again revived. Good things remained, as I recalled the strengths of our relationship rather than the bad times. I smiled to myself as the memories started to flood over me, and I chose to remember those good and precious things about my dad. As I got nearer to the plaque, I noticed that the bronze soldier's badge was gone. It had been stolen only two months after the grave had been placed there.

THINK ABOUT THIS:

Mine is not an explosive or dramatic story in many ways. It is the story of a dad who carried his unresolved pain from his past into his present. His actions and his ability to relate to his family at times reflected an inability to move past the negative experiences that had impacted him so deeply.

As his daughter, I was loved, and valued. As I look back, I know that now. But when I was a little girl, his actions and reactions often did not demonstrate that truth. Somehow, it all got stuck inside him, and he was unable

I was Alice looking through a warped looking glass, at the most important person in my life: God Himself.

to relay it to me. I got the wrong impression of who he really was on the inside. How often we allow that to happen in our relationships. How much we regret the unsaid when it is too late.

During my relationship with my dad I had formed my impression of who God was, how He would act towards me, and how he expected and wanted me to act. I saw my Heavenly Father through a window that was distorted. I was Alice looking through a warped looking glass, at the most important person in my life: God Himself. I did that because it was the only way I knew how. It wasn't until I lost my earthly dad that I was able to clearly find the relationship that was unfettered by past pain, grief and sadness. I had some insight into a father's relationship with a daughter, but there was much that was 'missing'.

Now I have discovered that comparison is no way to 'measure' my Heavenly Daddy. He is not only the creator of everything, but also the creator of me as an individual. His love for me is unfathomable. His heart for me is gigantic in capacity. His care for me is unceasing. And His calling to me when I did not know Him was constant, even relentless. And He is incomparable!

OVER TO YOU:

In some way perhaps, grief is a process that strengthens us. We can use the process and the crisis of grief to work through pain, giving birth to depth in our relationship with God, and to depth in our own character.

God's heart is for us and with us, and available at any time. He is not subject to past experience, and so is never 'up and down'. He's constant, dependable and is our Rock! Call Him, and He answers!

The love of our Heavenly Father can never be understood or quantified, humanly speaking. His nature is not the sum total of how things were with your earthly Dad, but a whole new relationship. If you use the human measure of earthly relationship to gauge and measure a supernatural one, it's a completely unbalanced equation!

He is immeasurable, limitless and waiting for you! It's your decision to accept and believe; indeed, to dance with Him.

Ecclesiastes 3:4 (NLT)

> A time to cry and a time to laugh.
> A time to grieve and a time to dance.

Psalm 30:11 (NLT)

> You have turned my mourning into joyful dancing.
> You have taken away my clothes of mourning and clothed me with joy,

---

Heavenly Father,

I am aware that I can spend my life regretting incidents and memories that make up some of who I am, or I can put to rest those memories and realize that you have everything that I need to become healed and also whole. I can lay them down and take up the newness of life that you promise in the Bible. Help me to do that today, Lord. Amen

EPILOGUE

This has been my story of a relationship that only lasted a short nineteen years. It has taken many years to recall and to record the memories that I have written. To reflect and respond to the lessons that came out of the memories has possibly taken even longer.

I am still finding information and historical reference to the circumstances of my dad's capture at St Valery en Caux, in the north of France. I have discovered that there were many soldiers of the 51st Highlanders who were similar to my dad, in that they too felt the abandonment of being surrendered as one of 10,000 men to the enemy as they desperately tried to defend their country and its people. Their hearts' cry must have all been for validation and recognition, but many instead lived with feelings of rejection and a lack of self-esteem. Historically, there are thousands of soldiers who could never fully adapt to life back home after life in the Prisoner of War camps during World War II. This post-war trauma played out, as in my father's life, in their peacetime relationships with loved ones in their families especially. But it also influenced, and in some cases damaged the next generation.

Much of life does not treat us the way we feel it should. We can only deal with our own personal disappointment and negative journey as the healing process is revealed to, and accepted by, each one of us. We can choose to accept and be made whole, or we can live in our world of sad memories that will hold us bound and ineffective whenever they choose to surface and restrict us. We can choose to remember the bad, or to major on the good!

I have found that reflection has a great deal to do with understanding. And getting time alone with my Dad in Heaven—that is, talking things through with Him—is the pathway to change. What that reflection has led me to is now an eternal relationship and love that will never end, never leave me, never cease to be the healing that is and continues to bring new life.

The Bible quotes Jesus as calling his Heavenly Father "Abba". This term is Aramaic (the language of the Middle East in Jesus' day) and a term that expresses a very close relationship with God. It is translated into our language as meaning "Daddy". (In some translations of the Bible it's "Papa").

Each time Jesus spoke the word "Abba" He demonstrated his complete trust and reliance on his Heavenly Father. He appealed to his Abba and he spoke of the authority that we have in God, that is, our Abba. And He gave us someone to come alongside us (See Galatians 4:6 below) to help us. This 'someone' is called the Holy Spirit. He can live in our hearts, and become our guide and our helper at any time. He does the will of the Father in Heaven, and is the Spirit of Jesus.

Romans 15-17 (The Message version)

This resurrection life you received from God is not a timid, grave-tending life. It's adventurously expectant, greeting God with a childlike "What's next, Papa?" God's Spirit touches our spirits and confirms who we really are. We know who he is, and we know who we are: Father and children. And we know we are going to get what's coming to us — an unbelievable inheritance! We go through exactly what Christ goes through. If we go through the hard times with him, then we're certainly going to go through the good times with him!

Galatians 4:6

Because you are his sons, God sent the Spirit of his Son into our hearts, the Spirit who calls out, "Abba, Father".

So you see, when you know this, it becomes easier to live as you were always meant to: with a joy and peace in your heart even though you may have been through difficult times and may be going through them right now.

It becomes easier to learn to act and respond in ways that you never thought you would, simply because you are learning a new way of living, and a new relationship. And it's not the same as an earthly one, because it's not natural, it's supernatural.

You are being guided and taught by the Spirit of Jesus. And no matter what your background, whether you have or had a father on the earth who was kind, gentle, loving or sad, depressed or even abusive, you can rise to be the daughter who has travelled the journey of your life towards health, happiness and wholeness with a constant loving Companion. You have travelled now to a new and bright, promising land with a future.

You have depended upon 'Abba'—'Daddy' in Heaven who loves you and wants to bless and heal you. And now you know that you are not a product of what has led up to this time, and you are not going to live that out in your future.

You are certainly a new creation!

YOUR NEXT STEP:

Perhaps you have decided whilst reading that you'd like to take some of the advice given, or see someone (a friend, pastor or counselor) to talk out those things that hold you back from experiencing not only wholeness in your life but *abundant blessing!* Maybe your journal will become your chosen way of communicating with your Heavenly Father; or perhaps a special place that you can go will become your vehicle to change things, as you chat to Jesus about the 'stuff' in your life that needs to be forgiven and redeemed.

This is the relationship that I now share with Jesus. It is the most natural thing in the world, to step out when I feel Him extend his hand, and hear him say,

"Come, let's dance".

I often hear a familiar strain that drifts towards me on the night air when I am alone, looking up at the stars. Its unmistakable melody draws me in as I approach my Daddy's presence at any time, in any place. It is welcoming, and makes me feel as though I'm 'home'. It comes from that place in which I am aware of His peace, where I am at once both settled and free. My future holds promise and the journey is very much worth it..

And my Daddy is just a prayer away.

Heavenly Father,

As I close my eyes, I can visualize you holding out your hand to me. Help me to bravely take it, to come alongside you, and to know that you will never let me go. Help me to dance with you forever, by believing, accepting and enjoying you. Amen.

TO ORDER MORE COPIES

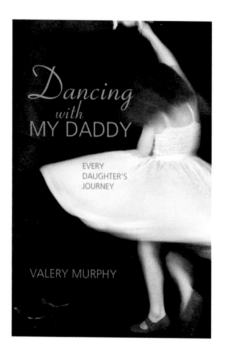

For more information about ordering copies of this book,

and for discount information for large orders, go to:

www.influenceresources.com